EARTHCHANGE

EARTHCHANGE

by Clare Cooper

Lerner Publications Company • Minneapolis

q

This edition first published in the United States by Lerner
Publications Company, 1986. Original edition published by
Hodder & Stoughton Children's Books, London, 1985.

Manufactured in the United States of America

LIBRARY OF CONGRESS CATALOGING-IN-PUBLICATION DATA

Cooper, Clare.
    Earthchange.

    Summary: After a catastrophe turns Earth into an
inhospitable wilderness, young Rose sets out to find
help for her grandmother and a baby, warding off
wolves and fierce humans, and finally reaching a group
of survivors with scientific interests in restoring
Earth to its original beauty.
    [1. Survival—Fiction. 2. Man—Influence on nature—
Fiction. 3. Environmental protection—Fiction]
I. Title. II. Title: Earth change.
PZ7.C78473Ear 1986   [Fic]   85-24028
ISBN 0-8225-0730-7 (lib. bdg.)

1 2 3 4 5 6 7 8 9 10 96 95 94 93 92 91 90 89 88 87 86

Hoy

Contents

Contents

1
Secrets

There was a hill in the distance, far away across the misty plain. It stood alone. A tower had been built on its summit.

Rose couldn't see the hill from Camp. She could only see it if she crept away, between the tall, rusting towers, over the rows of buckled rails, beneath the sagging, snapping wires and through the twisted fence, to the hummock with the pine tree on it. She crept there as often as she dared.

She loved looking at the hill. She would stand with her back against the rough bark of the pine tree, listening to the whispering in its three remaining branches, shading her eyes from the glare in the sky, just looking at the hill.

She would have liked to find out about it, to ask: "Has it got a name? Does anybody live there? Is it a special place?" But she wasn't supposed to have seen the hill, or even to know that it was there, so she couldn't ask. She could only wonder.

Grandmother was the only one who knew that Rose had seen it. Luckily, when she first went walking and found the hummock, Grandmother was the first one she had told. If she had told any of the others she would have been in dreadful trouble, Grandmother said.

"You're not supposed to go walking," Grandmother had whispered, pulling her down on to her pile of wolf skins. "Don't ever let anybody know that you go walking," she had warned. But she didn't say "Don't ever go walking," Rose noticed, so she didn't stop walking to the hummock. She simply made quite sure that no one ever saw her creep out of Camp or slink back in again. She didn't even tell Grandmother when she had been walking, though she was sure that Grandmother always knew. Grandmother would always smile her secret smile when she saw her come in from walking, but they didn't whisper about it.

It was sensible not to whisper if they didn't really need to, because they had another, more important, secret which they had to whisper about, and that was that Grandmother had a book hidden in Camp, and, even more secret, that she had taught Rose to read.

This was a deadly secret. Rose wouldn't let herself think about what the rest of them in Camp would do to her and Grandmother if they found out about it.

"No good comes out of books," Boss said. That was Rules. Boss had found some books once, as he and Joe and Eddie were pulling stone from one of the ruins to patch up a hole in the hut where Marilyn went to live before Baby was born. They never bothered with the ruins except when they needed stone, it was too much hard work. But when Boss found the books, hidden there beneath the rubble, he and the others had all gone mad for a while, and had rushed around tearing at beams and girders that they couldn't hope to move, crazy to find every one of the hated books that had dared to lurk there ever since the Old Days.

They had burnt them all at the next storm, throwing them at the Sparking Place, and shrieking with excitement as each poor, shapeless lump of sodden pulp flared in the intense heat and fell to Earth, shattering into a thousand sparks and embers.

They weren't even real books any more, either, Rose

thought now, as she crept beneath the Sparking Place on her way back from the hummock. I wonder what Boss and the others would feel like if they could burn Grandmother's *real* book. Would it make them even more excited if it was a real book? Would they look inside it to see what it was like before they burnt it? Surely if they did they would see how beautiful it was, and then let her keep it so that I could read it to them too.

Rose often wondered about this. Grandmother said that Boss would burn it with even greater pleasure if he saw the pictures and the colours and the beautiful neatness of it all.

"Why is Boss like that?" Rose had asked again and again. Grandmother always answered in much the same way. "Because that's the way his father taught him to be. Just my luck it is! Just my luck to choose a nice, bright, young scientist who loves all the things I love, and then get mixed up with a hulking great contrary moron like Boss's father, who couldn't even put two thoughts together, let alone read," Grandmother always said.

Tomorrow we might get a chance to read, Rose thought now. Tomorrow when Boss and all of them go off all day to fish and we are left with Baby. Tomorrow, Grandmother will take the book out from the bag inside her skirt where she's got it hidden at the moment, and, when I've done my work, I'll read to her.

Rose loved the book. *The Wind in the Willows,* she thought. She knew all about the wind, but she had only seen pictures of willow trees in the book. She often wondered about willows, but what she wondered about most of all in the book was how anyone, especially a *man,* could have made up a book about all those animals as though they were people.

Rose had never seen a mole, or a toad, or a badger, or

an otter, or a field mouse, or a hedgehog, or a stoat or
weasel. Grandmother said that there might not be any of
them left any more, since Everything Went Wrong. Rats
Rose did know about. She couldn't understand how anyone could bear to imagine about a rat, though Grandmother did say that Ratty was a water rat and they were
different. But still a rat. Rose knew *all* about rats. She
knew about ferrets, too. Boss had a lot of ferrets. Now
that he couldn't hunt wolves properly any more, he
caught rats with his ferrets, when it was too rough to
fish, to feed everyone in Camp. Rose knew *all* about
rats. There were even more rats than there were wolves...
Rose shuddered.

Quickly, she thought about the book again, and of
cuddling up against Grandmother's thin, warm side
among the wolf skins. The book had been Grandmother's
prize at school in the Old Days. Grandmother had told
Rose about school, where there were hundreds of children. Fancy! *Hundreds* of children! There had been *three*
children in Camp once. There had been Rory and Jessica
as well as Rose. But Rory had caught a cough. He hadn't
lasted once he caught that cough. And Jessica had been
caught out in a storm—no one lasted, caught out in a
storm—so now there was only Rose and Baby.

If Baby lasted. If they could trust him when he could
talk, then they would teach him to read too, and then he
and Rose would be almost like a small school, Grandmother said. Grandmother had loved school. At school
Grandmother had been teacher's pet.

"What is a pet?" Rose had had to ask.

"A favorite animal," Grandmother had tried to explain,
"an animal that you love and take care of and that loves
you back and takes care of you," she had told her, but
Rose couldn't imagine loving an animal.

She heard a movement ahead of her, a scuttling, scrabbling on the metal side of the next tower. Instantly she stood still, turning her head, quickly, towards the sound. Rats! She had known it would be. Rats, running from their city inside the center of that battered, rusting ruin of a tower. Rats running away—why? Was that tower falling down? No. It looked no nearer collapse than it usually did. So why were they running? There could only be one reason. Boss was there, Boss with his ferrets...Boss. She would have to be careful.

Rose forgot the rats. Boss! And here she was walking! She crouched down, and scrambled on her hands and feet, low behind a patch of long-dead balsam, then waited, watching for him fearfully.

There he was! Boss! Busy with his catch. Good! He wouldn't see her if he was busy. All she had to do was wait. But what was that among the dead flowers? A ferret! His best, white ferret! He would look for it. He would come to look for it, and stoop to pick it up, and he would find her and know that she had been walking.

He did look for it. Rose heard him grunt with irritation as he glanced at the row of ferret bags and saw that one was open at the neck. She watched helplessly, shivering, as she saw him catch sight of the ferret and begin to limp towards the place where she was hiding. Run! She would run. She could out-run everyone in Camp. But he would still see her. There would still be a settling-up, later. Better to stay there, to be caught, to get it over. Closer...closer...nearly here...

Rose cringed closer to the earth as Boss reached out. And then the Sparking Place began to hiss.

It saved her. Boss stopped abruptly and looked up at the place where the sagging cables ended in a cluster of small, broken, upturned bowls, like clenched, brown fists, high on two upright rails between two towers. Rose saw his stupid eyes gleam, and his thick lips curl into his awful, sneering smile. "Storm!" he said.

The Sparking Place always hissed before a storm. Next, it would crackle, and then bright, jagged lightning would leap between its fists.

And, after that, the Voice would begin, and they would all go down into the Hole, below the tallest tower, and listen to it. And then they would wail.

Boss loved the coming of a storm... Rose dreaded it.

2
The Voice and The Wailing

"Hurry! Hurry, girl! Hurry!" Marilyn pushed Rose out through the doorway of the hut with a well-placed shove from her bony shoulder. Marilyn had bullied Rose ever since she had become Mother. Being Mother was special. Even more special when you were the *only* Mother. She barged into Sharon who was going to be Mother, too, soon. Marilyn didn't like Sharon any more.

She pushed and chivied Rose along the stone path to the Hole, with Baby, wrapped in the softest skins, in her arms. Everyone had to listen to the Voice during the storm. Everyone had to wail. Boss's Rules. Everyone, that is, except Grandmother, who couldn't move far from her bed, even with her sticks, because of what she called her Thritis. Sometimes Rose longed to be old and to have the Thritis, no matter how painful it was. Anything would be better than having to listen to the Voice and having to wail.

"Now, *you* are going to hold Baby this time." Marilyn's shrill voice jarred in her ear. "Sit at the back, and keep him quiet. Here!" She handed Rose a small bone, chewed bare, gleaming white. "Shove this in his mouth if he as much as whimpers, and don't let him scream. He ruined it all for me last time. Ruined it!"

Rose was amazed that anything, even the lusty yelling Baby had given forth last storm, could ruin Marilyn's pleasure in listening to the Voice and wailing.

Marilyn seemed to guess what she was thinking. "*And it made Boss mad,*" she said spitefully. She knew that that would make Rose do what she wanted.

When they climbed down into the Hole, the bright spot of light which brought the Voice was already shining from the middle of the dull, grey window which seemed to look out on nowhere from the middle of the wall. It was a dreadful spot, that light. Things seemed to move in it, things which Rose couldn't really see but which reminded her of grubs crawling in a rotten apple. She was supposed to stare at that spot of light as she listened to the Voice. Boss's Rules. Boss, with his crippled leg stretched out uncomfortably, sat right in front of the grey window, in the place of honor. Joe and Eddie were squatting on the floor on either side of him. All three were staring at the spot. All three were already half entranced by it.

Rose sat with her back against the wall just inside the doorway and tried to cuddle Baby, but he wouldn't lie still. He was growing quite big now. He liked to sit up and see what was happening around him. Marilyn thought it might soon be safe to give him a name. She was sure that he was going to last. But Grandmother said that the Baby before him had been older than he was when it went, and the one before that had even been able to stand up, but it still hadn't lasted. Rose knew that Grandmother didn't think that this one would last either. "Boss shouldn't have said eat that cow," Grandmother said. "We should have kept the cow for milk. There are plenty of wild bulls around. We might have managed a calf every year."

But they had eaten the cow. Rose could only just remember it, a huge, shaggy, white animal with horns and a terrible kick. It had kicked Boss and broken his leg.

Boss couldn't run now, or even walk properly—but he was still Boss.

Rose watched the three remaining women climb down past her. Joyce was kind. Joyce had been her mother's sister. She smiled at Rose as she crawled past. The other two were not so friendly. Molly never smiled, but then, she was always ill. She had a terrible cough, like Rory's. Pat was just bad-tempered. Pat had been Mother twice, but both her babies had gone quickly.

Baby began to bounce on Rose's lap. She held him tightly. Grandmother could be wrong about this one. He was strong even though he was so thin. He gurgled noisily, and she saw Marilyn twist around and scowl at her. Where was that bone? She found it just as the Voice began.

Grandmother knew more about the Voice than anyone else in Camp, but she wouldn't even whisper to Rose about it. It was a secret which she wouldn't share. She *had* whispered about the dull, gray window, though. She could remember when, in the Old Days, there had been hundreds of dull, gray windows like that, fixed on to the fronts of boxes. They had been called Telly in the Old Days. They had shown pictures. Grandmother whispered that the Telly in the Hole was worse than useless, that it was the flat, gray box beside it that was really important. That box had been called Video in the Old Days. The Voice came from the flat, gray Video box, not from the bright spot of light.

But it didn't matter where the Voice came from. Nor did the Voice matter either, really. It was not really the Voice that they had to come here for. It was really the wailing.

Boss loved the wailing. Grandmother whispered that Boss was secretly beginning to believe that the wailing would make Things Go Right again. Grandmother whispered that it wouldn't be long before Boss began to take presents to the Voice when he came to wail. That it wouldn't be long before he began to make sacrifices...

. But the Voice had begun. What was it going to say this time? Rose knew by heart a lot of the words the Voice said. Some of them brought on the wailing more quickly than others. What was it saying this time? She listened. "...we thought we had a hundred years in which to..."

"Aw!" It was near the place where it whistled and whirred and hummed. The whistling, whirring and humming brought on terrible wailing. The wailing was going to be unbearable this storm...And here it came! *Now* she must keep Baby quiet.

The problem, Rose knew, was that Baby was afraid of the wailing. It terrified him. It had terrified her until she grew used to it. At first, Baby had slept through it. But now he didn't sleep. He sat wide awake. And last time he had screamed.

Grandmother had said, "Leave him with me," but Boss had made the Rule.

Everyone must listen to the Voice. And listening meant wailing. Everyone must wail...

The wail began. Boss began it. "Aah...ah...uuh ...uh...ahh...ah," he began. Marilyn joined in, then Eddie. Soon every head in front of Rose was swaying rhythmically, all together, to and fro. Then the shoulders. "Aah...uh...uuh...ahhh...ah..." Marilyn jerked her head until her long, matted hair swung like seaweed in the tide. Boss shook his fists above his head, punching at the air. Sharon began to wave her hands, limply, aimlessly. "Aah...uh...ah...uh..."

Baby turned his frightened little face to Rose. He was going to scream. Where was that bone? She felt his fist and groped around in her lap. Ugh! He had wetted her. She heard him whimper. Where was that bone? There! On the floor!

Rose was on her knees with Baby clasped beneath her when the television on the wall exploded. The searing blast of air ripped above her head. The door behind her splintered outwards. For a moment, a very brief moment, there was no noise... then, another explosion. A sheet of flame... One scream...

The door! She must reach the door! With a scrabble and a leap and a twist of thin, hard limbs, Rose was out through the door with Baby in her arms. Another explosion sent her reeling out into the storm, out across the patch of rubble-strewn mud, towards the hut and Grandmother. Behind her, the tower and the Sparking Place toppled to Earth with a thunder which stifled every other sound.

3
Grandmother's Decision

"Just my luck!" Grandmother said. "Just my luck! I get rid of the wailing and Boss but everybody else goes too. Just my luck!"

"We can read the book all day now," Rose said.

"So we can!" Grandmother screwed up her face into a mask of withered wrinkles, the way she did when she was pleased about something secret. She fumbled in her clothes, and produced the book with a flourish. "Tan-tan-tara!" She made her trumpet sound.

Trumpets were music, so was singing. "We can sing too, now," Rose said.

They sang all evening, and read the book, and took it in turns to chew pieces of smoked meat soft enough for Baby to eat.

"It's lucky Marilyn had begun to wean him," Grandmother said, "or we'd have real problems. Boss shouldn't have said eat that cow, though. He shouldn't have said eat that cow."

Rose went to bed feeling happier than she could remember ever feeling before. She snuggled up against Grandmother's back and relaxed. It was a pity about Joyce, but she didn't care about the others, and she was *glad* that Boss was gone—Boss and the wailing. And now I can read and sing all day, she thought as she drifted off to sleep. She roused for a moment when she remembered the fishing. "I'll have to do the fishing tomorrow." She didn't like the waves. Sometimes a wave rolled in that was much bigger than the others. Her father had been drowned in the waves. Could you go the way your father went? Grandmother had never said that you could. You went the way your mother went, Grandmother said. I'll be all right in the waves, Rose thought, and fell asleep.

Grandmother didn't sleep well that night. Rose woke several times to hear her moaning gently to herself. Baby moaned too. He was missing his mother. Rose knew all about missing a mother. But why is Grandmother moaning? she wondered.

Grandmother was quiet as Rose stoked the fire and fetched the handful of withered apples with which they usually began their day. Baby had to have his chewed for him again. Rose waited until it was Grandmother's turn to chew, then began to talk about the fishing.

"I know how to do it," she said. "I'll manage."

"You're not going fishing," Grandmother said. She didn't look at Rose. She was pretending to be concentrating on Baby, but Rose knew that she wasn't. "You're not going fishing," she said again. "There's something else you're going to do today."

"Not ratting! Please, not ratting!" Rose began to wail.

"Stop that! No wailing now. No more Boss, no more wailing. That's a new Rule!" Grandmother said sharply, and went on chewing for a moment.

Rose sat quietly, waiting to hear what she was going to say. It was going to be something awful. She knew it. It might not be ratting, but it was still going to be awful.

"You're going to go for a walk," Grandmother said.

Rose couldn't believe it. There was nothing awful about going for a walk, not now that Boss wasn't there to find out about it. And yet Grandmother said it as though it was going to be awful.

"It will be a long walk," Grandmother said. "It will take you about a week. You'll leave Baby here with me." She sighed and bent her head low over the tiny, thin child as she said that. "I'll tell you exactly what to do, and how to do it. And I'll tell you where to go."

"Where?" Rose asked. "Where shall I walk to?"

"To the hill," Grandmother said. "You see, Rose, we can't last here, like this, all alone. So, you're going to walk to the hill to get help."

4
Rose Gets Ready

Rose did exactly as Grandmother told her. "First of all," Grandmother said, "go to Marilyn's hut and bring back all the food and skins and tools and anything useful that you can find."

Rose enjoyed rummaging around in Marilyn's hut. Marilyn would have been furious! And what a lot of apples she had there. *And* some of those plum things Eddie had found. They were supposed to be all gone! The cheat! Rose thought. Then she changed her mind. No. Marilyn had been Mother. Mothers you fed as well as you could and took care of. Marilyn was allowed all that fruit. All the same, it was satisfying to think that she wouldn't get it now. She filled Marilyn's cracked china bowl, and carried it back to Grandmother.

Then she went back for the wolf skins and a tall, faded, red jug that she had never seen before. Marilyn must have found that washed up on the beach after a big wave. It had lasted well. She had stacks of driftwood too. Grandmother hadn't mentioned wood for her fire, but she would need a lot to keep her and Baby warm for a week.

"I'll bring you all her wood, too," Rose said, as she piled the first armful up against the wall as near to the fire as she thought would be safe. "I'll bring you every stick I can find," she said.

Grandmother simply grunted, and began to divide the fruit and the smoked meat into two piles. One was bigger

than the other. Rose thought that was the pile for Grandmother and Baby. But when Grandmother said, "Now
fetch that satchel Boss kept for fishing," and she had
fetched it, Grandmother began to stow away the biggest
pile inside it.

"Is that for me to take?" Rose said. "But you'll need
more than me."

"Hush-up!" Grandmother told her sharply. "You're
just like your grandfather, always arguing. Of course we
won't need more than you. We'll be lying here, in the
warm, and you'll be out there, on the go in the bitter
cold. You'll need the most. Now, go and fetch those
rooty cakey things Joyce made yesterday," she said, and
while Rose went to look for them she quickly pushed
more fruit from her own pile into the satchel. "You can
take all the nuts," she told her. "Nuts is no good for us,
with me with only five teeth in my head and him with
none. You'll need a cup. Take mine, it's bigger than
yours. And now let's sort out the skins."

Eddie had been good at skinning wolves, much better
than Boss and the others. His skins had no holes in
them, and were fine and supple and completely clean.
Rose was already dressed in a tunic and long boots
made of skin. Now Grandmother chose another big skin,
and tied it around her waist for extra warmth, and found
one with part of the head, including the ears, still at-
tached, which she fastened around Rose's shoulders so
that the wolf head made a hood which would keep most
of her own head warm.

Grandmother chuckled. "I wouldn't like to meet you
in the half light," she said. "A right old turn you'd give
me, that's for sure, if I didn't know it was you. Now, sit
down and I'll tell you how to go about this walk."

"Not yet," Rose said. "I haven't got your water yet.

You'll need lots of water. I'll fill everything I can find, and you make sure you make it last a week."

Grandmother's lips trembled, and she busied herself, quickly, with Baby.

When Rose was satisfied that every old plastic bowl, bucket and jug that lay around Camp was filled to overflowing from the stream, she sat down at the foot of Grandmother's bed and listened to her instructions.

"When you leave here in a minute, you are *not* to come back, Rose, unless you have help with you," Grandmother said. "That is a Rule. No whys nor wherefores. That is a Rule. Do you understand?"

Rose nodded. She didn't understand why, but she knew all about Rules. Grandmother must be taking over from Boss, though she couldn't hope to be as terrifying, thank heavens.

"First of all, you will set the ferrets free, every one of them. They'll look after themselves from now on."

"Won't we need them when I come back?"

"No, we won't need them no more," Grandmother said, and went on quickly. "After that, you're going to need to watch for other Camps."

"Other Camps!" Rose was amazed. "I thought there was only one Camp."

"No, there isn't only one Camp. There are a lot of other Camps around here. *Don't go anywhere near them.* They're—they're not nice. If you see or hear anyone while you're still near here, hide or run, whichever you think best. You'll have to decide that for yourself."

"Are there other Bosses, then?" Rose began to shake. She bit her knuckle, and tried not to feel afraid at this new, terrifying widening of her world.

"Yes, there are other Bosses—and worse animals to keep an eye open for. There are wild bulls on the plain, and wolves at night, of course, and I expect there might be bears. I'm pretty sure the zoos let bears out when they let out the wolves. Some of them could have survived the snow." Grandmother seemed to be thinking carefully. "The lions and tigers, and the other big cats would have found it all too much for them, poor devils, but the bears would have been used to the cold, perhaps—yes, it's wolves and bears you'll have to watch out for."

She had to describe a bear, for Rose had never even seen a picture of one. And then she said, "Now, Rose, we've come to the important part of what you have to do. You have to begin your walk by way of the hummock and the pine tree. There's another secret there—a secret of your grandfather's," she said.

Then Grandmother held Rose's hand, and pulled her close to her, and told her how, when Things first Went Wrong, she and Grandfather had liked to walk together to the hummock and look at the hill across the flat lands. "At night there was a light on the tower," she said. "The only light on Earth, I used to think it was. I used to say it was magic, but Grandfather saw more in it than that. He knew something about that light, but he wouldn't tell me what it was, no matter how much I asked. He would just say, 'There's people over there, Rosy. If the snow hadn't come when it did I'd have taken you there years ago and if anything goes wrong here I want you to go there with my lad.' He meant, if he was killed, I knew he did, but, later, when he *was* killed, and was gone, I still had your father a baby, and I wanted him to last. He would have died if I'd taken him out into the snow. And afterwards, when he was bigger and the snow had stopped, well, *somebody* had to try to undo some of the stupid harm the Boss was doing at Camp, so I stayed, and I never even tried to get to the hill," she said.

Then Grandmother told Rose that Grandfather had hidden things in a secret hole in the hummock, things which would have helped her reach the hill safely if she had tried to go. "There's his survival bag, that he took when he went walking on the mountains in the Old Days," she said. "It's a big bag to keep him warm and dry if he got lost and had to lie around all night. You must sleep in that. That's an important Rule, Rose," she said firmly. "And there's his knife in there, too. You must sharpen that and keep it sharp and use it if you have to. It'd kill a wolf, Grandfather reckoned. And— and there's a picture of him, too. I had to take that with me when I went, he said, though he wouldn't tell me why, so *you* take it with *you*," she told Rose.

And then Grandmother tied a knot in the strap on the satchel to shorten it so that it rested comfortably on Rose's hip, and told her never to walk unless she could see the hill in front of her. "Or you'll get lost," she said, "and it'd be just my luck for you to get lost, and me left here with my eyes too bad to read my own book and nothing to do but chew apples and rat meat for that Baby. Use your common sense, and sing as you go, my sweet, brave Rose and remember: No Boss, no wailing—and no Boss *talk* either. When you get there remember to talk like *I* taught you, like in the book, *not* like Boss, remember...Now!" Grandmother pushed Rose away from her roughly. "Off you go! Tan-tan-tara!" she sang...and pointed at the door.

And Rose began her walk to the hill.

5
The Secret Beneath the Pine Tree

The ferrets were no problem. As Rose slid back each wooden latch and let each cage door drop downwards with a clatter, they leapt past her to their freedom, bounding in long, curving springs across the mud towards the nearest tower. She hurried away before she could be forced to witness their first murderous on-slaught on that citadel of rats.

It was strange walking to the hummock with no fear of being seen, to walk upright, looking around, instead of scuttling from one shadow to the next, watching for Boss or the others. She had never noticed quite how rusted away the towers were, or how precariously they swayed and tilted in the fierce wind that blew in from the sea. She hurried past them, looking towards the lone pine tree and, behind it, to the bright, white sky.

Grandmother had told her where to look for the secret. It lay beneath a flat stone on the Camp side of the tree. The stone was covered with a thin layer of mud and a few, straggling grass roots. Rose pulled away the grass roots gently, taking care not to break them. You never broke grass roots, never. Rules! The stone had become embedded, but not too deeply. Just a little digging and scratching with her nails and she could get her fingers beneath one edge. She pulled and tugged, bracing her back against the tree, and the stone squelched upwards. She rested it against the trunk and knelt beside the hole.

It was a shallow hole, lined with a sealed, metal box.

The transparent survival bag and the long, straight, double-bladed knife were wrapped in some soft material which felt greasy but wasn't. They were quite dry—and so was the picture.

With curiosity, and the sort of tenderness she felt for Grandmother, Rose looked at her grandfather's face. He didn't have a beard! She had never seen a clean-shaven man before. She rubbed the tip of her finger over the brown cheek of the man in the photograph, as though she was feeling the smoothness of the real face. He's smiling like Grandmother does! She had never seen a man smile like that. And he *did* like hills and books and singing. She could see that it was true. Grandmother had always told her that he did. Now she could see it in his eyes.

She wiped off the smear of mud that her finger had made, and turned the picture over. Writing always went with pictures, as far as she knew. Yes! There was some writing. Just two words. "J...a...ck," she read. "Jack." That was Grandfather's name, Jack. Grandmother had told her so. But what was the other word? "G...i... bb...s, Gibbs." That was a new one. It looked like another name. Did people have two names before Everything Went Wrong? Rose didn't know.

She opened the fish satchel and tucked the picture carefully down beside the food, then shielded it from possible stains and scratches with the survival bag. The knife she sharpened on the flat stone lid of the secret place. She tested the point and the edge on the ball of her thumb, as she had seen Boss test his knife. It was sharper than the knife Eddie used to skin wolves, much sharper. She was satisfied that Grandfather had been right about it. With it she could kill—if she *could* kill...She didn't quite know what to do with it then. Would it be sensible to carry it? She thought she might feel safer with it ready in her hand, but Boss had been funny about weapons in people's hands. If he saw anyone with just a stick he always tended to attack, to get the person before the person got him, Grandmother said. Possibly other Bosses would behave in just the same way. Rose thought about it for a while, and then decided to lay the knife on top of the survival bag, just inside the satchel, with the flap unfastened, so that she could reach the knife as soon as she needed it.

After that she stood up and looked at the hill. The freezing mist over the plain was thin today, after the storm. It lay, the thinnest of white sheets, close above the levels. In the distance the hill rose above it, thrusting upwards into the bright, clean air. Until that day, Rose had always gazed and dreamed whenever she walked to see the hill. Now, she looked at it differently. Grandmother had said that she must use her common sense. So would she be able to see the hill when she stepped down from the hummock? Was the freezing mist as thin as it seemed? And where were these other Camps?

Now that she knew that the other Camps were there, Rose found that she looked at that view with a much greater awareness of what she was seeing. Away to the right, she could see one thin, gray wisp of smoke rising vertically as far as the line of the mist, where it flattened abruptly in a perfect right-angle and then disappeared into the general cloudiness.

Rose drew in her breath with a hiss. A Camp right there! So close! She looked away from it, to the vast stretch of ruins on the left of the view, ruins which she had seen so many times before, but never looked at as she looked at them today. More smoke! More Camps! Camps everywhere! She began to feel that she would never avoid them all, but then, as she looked, it seemed to her that there was one, clear path. I'll keep straight down the middle, she decided, and stood still for a moment longer, planning the first part of her route.

Between her and the hill, in the straight line which she had chosen, stood a clump of wind-swept trees and something squat, that looked as though it could be another hummock. She would head for the trees first, and then the hummocky thing, and when she got there she would plan the next part of the walk.

She shut the box, but didn't lay the stone back over it. There was no point. There was no need for secrets in *this* Camp any more. She did look back once, but wished that she hadn't, for it made her want to go back, and Grandmother had said that she mustn't. "Not until I come back with help. Rules!" she told herself. Then she swung the satchel over her shoulder and stepped down on to the mud of the plain.

6
The Golden Hound

Rose ran, and even skipped at first, excited by so much happening so quickly, but she soon settled down to a steady march, singing, as Grandmother had said she should. *"Jack and Jill,"* she sang.

Jack and Jill went up the hill to fetch a pail of water,
Jack fell down and broke his crown, and Jill came
*   tumbling after.*
But Jack and Rose, I will suppose, climb up the hill in
*   laughter,*
They laugh and sing till the steeples ring, and live
*   happily ever after.*

It was one of Grandfather's songs. It fitted nicely to her marching steps. She sang it again. Grandmother always explained about Grandfather's songs. In this one Jill wasn't anyone in particular, Grandmother said, but Jack was Grandfather, and *this* Rose was Grandmother herself.

Suddenly, as she neared the trees, Rose realized that she should have been being careful. A large, hump-backed bull loomed, close, in the mist. It grazed, tearing at the bark. It hadn't noticed her.

She stopped and stood quite still, her heart beating rapidly. What should she do? She had never been so close to a bull before. And she was so close that she could count its ribs. Huge ribs! It was thinner than Baby! Its shoulder blades seemed about to thrust through its mud-caked skin. And its horns! Look at its horns!

The bull raised its head. Rose stopped breathing. She stood, motionless, as the bull snuffed at the air. It could smell her. It knew she was there. Still she stood. It grazed again.

Very slowly, Rose retreated backwards until the huge bulk of the animal faded into the mist again. Then she ran. On her toes she went, away to the left. The bull had been facing the other way. It mustn't turn. It mustn't hear her. It mustn't smell her again.

But it did smell her. It must have, for something disturbed it, and there was nothing else in that vast field of mud and scrub except Rose and the bull. She heard it bellow, but couldn't interpret the sound. Was it a question noise...or a challenge...or was it a chase noise? She didn't know. She turned sharply left to where she thought the trees must be and ran. She thought she heard its hoof beats behind her. She glanced back. It wasn't there. Relief! The trees appeared, dimly, ahead. She glanced around again. It *was* there—not behind her but beside, heading for her, trotting, snorting. It broke into a gallop. Rose dashed among the trees and dodged behind one thick, grey trunk and then another and then stood still as the bull thundered past. Then she climbed. Quickly she swung and scrambled into the tree's lowest branches, and clung there, watching, as the bull barged around, snorting and pawing at the soft earth.

After a while it began to tear at bark again, and she had to wait until it wandered back out into open country. It seemed to Rose that she waited all day. She began to fret. She had meant to walk so far that day, and now here she was trapped right beside Camp. She felt cross with herself. She should have been more careful. She should have seen the bull sooner and avoided it. And what if it had been a Boss that she had met like that and not a bull! She couldn't think about that. She wouldn't. She looked around at the trees.

Trees close together were a wood, Grandmother said. Was this a Wild Wood like in the book, with stoats and weasels and ferrets and the terror if they saw you and watched you with their little, pointed faces peering from every shadow, and whistling all around you? And she would never find Badger's front door! No! That was a story, she told herself firmly. But there might be *real* ferrets and things. She would still have to be careful.

As soon as the bull seemed safely out of sight, she climbed down to Earth again and began to creep, steadily and silently, between the trees, peering furtively into the dark shadows. It wasn't long before she found a path. She stopped then, to think again.

A path meant that either large animals or people, or both, came that way often. Was it safe to use it? Walking on the path would be easier than picking her way among the trees with their exposed roots and low branches. But was it safe? She decided that it was worth risking — if she was careful.

She began to walk again, avoiding twigs and loose stones, alert for the slightest movement, so she saw the next animal even before it saw her. It was harmless, anyway, whatever it was, that was only too obvious. It was hanging in a tree, caught around its shoulders by the sort of snare Boss had used to catch wolves. But it wasn't a wolf. Whatever was it?

Rose walked up to it slowly. It would make a good skin, one of the best! It was covered with thick, creamy-golden hair, but its ears were black. It was a very beautiful animal. Someone had a good catch there! But what was it?

It growled as she moved close, and then writhed and kicked, frantic to escape. Rose stood still and stared at it, and the animal kept still as well. It began to pant painfully. "I do believe you are a dog," Rose told it. There were no dogs in Camp, but Grandmother had had one once. There was a dog in the book too. Dogs, Rose knew, were pets. Pets shouldn't be caught in snares. Grandmother says, pets are for looking after and loving, she thought, and then she noticed the dog's swollen teats, dripping with milk. It's a *Mother* dog. It's got a Baby it should be feeding.

Rose was worried. Mothers were important. Babies must be fed. Rules. Boss's Rules *and* Grandmother's too, for once. Rose obeyed. Quickly, she slipped the satchel from her shoulder, put it down behind a tree, and took out the long knife. She would have to cut down this dog and set it free.

The dog knew about knives. As soon as it saw this one it began to yelp with fear, squirming and writhing and snapping at her hand as she reached up towards the rope. She couldn't get near enough to cut it down. It would bite her face or her arm.

Wolf bites made you mad, Boss said. Did dog bites make you mad? Rose hesitated. No! She had to help it. "Keep still, stupid dog," she snarled at it. She would have to hold it still, get around behind it, hold it by its tail. It couldn't kick backwards like the cow had kicked. "Hold still!" she snarled at it again, and reached up, standing on her toes. Twice she had to leap away quickly as its teeth snapped against her arm. The third time she gripped it firmly at the root of its tail and slashed wildly above its head.

The knife cut the rope as effortlessly as if she had been cutting a hair. She leapt back as the dog fell, snapping, at her feet. She expected it to attack her, and backed against a tree, brandishing her knife, but all it did was lie there, panting and whining quietly. Is it hurt, or is it tired out? Rose watched it. Tired and thirsty, she decided. She could hear water running somewhere among the trees. She rummaged in the satchel for the cup, then followed the sound and found a deep ditch with a small stream trickling along at the very bottom of it. She slid down, filled her cup, and took it back, brimming, for the dog.

This time, as she came near, the dog didn't snap. It looked at her suspiciously, as it if doubted her good intentions, but licked its lips and eyed the water eagerly. Rose held out the cup slowly, taking care not to startle it. It drank the cup dry, then looked at her in the way Baby looked when he expected more. Rose filled the cup again, and this time as it drank, she eased the noose of the snare undone. It slid to the path.

When the dog had emptied the cup again it heaved itself painfully to its feet, and stood there as though it was feeling its limbs and its neck, testing them for pain. It wasn't as big as a wolf. It came up to just above her knees. It had long legs for its size, longer than a wolf's.

Suddenly the dog raised its head. Its black ears turned back and lay open against its long, thin head. Its nose twitched. It could hear something. Next moment Rose could hear it too — a voice, voices. There were men coming.

Quickly the dog turned away from her and moved into the shelter of the trees, hurrying stiffly, intent on escaping from these men. Rose heard the voices again. They were close. She looked at the dog retreating purposefully. It would be going to its Baby. And if Mother dogs were anything like every other Mother Rose knew about this one would have the safest, most comfortable place she could find for that Baby. And what had Grandmother said about pets? If you take care of pets they take care of you. Right! This dog could share its den with her. They would both be safe together.

She grabbed the satchel, and, slipping the strap over her head, ran after the dog with the knife still in her hand. Behind her, far too close, she heard the men exclaim angrily as they found the cut rope.

And then came a new, worse, danger. As she heard the men cry out, Rose heard, too, the first crash of thunder of a new storm and saw the sky ahead of her burn with the white heat of sheet lightning. Storm! Of course, storm! She hadn't been thinking. Nor had Grandmother! So much else had happened they hadn't thought about yesterday's storm. It had been a *dry* storm. After one dry storm came two wet. This was a Three Storm Group. It had been months since they had a Three Storm Group. This would be a bad one. They were always bad when you had had months free of them. There would be a deluge of rain and hail, then a lull, and then hour after hour of thunder, lightning, rain and hail. And then the wind would come, the strong wind, the wind that whirled, that lifted trees and sides of huts away. The wind that had taken Jessica. Children went, if they were caught in a storm. And a Three Storm Group would kill a Boss.

Rose bent low and ran like a hunter. She mustn't lose that dog. Sheltering in the dog's den was the only way she could survive.

7

The Torrent

The dog wouldn't let her in! Rose followed it along the ditch, running through the stream and up the stone bank on the far side, to a hole that must, at some time in the Old Days, have been a drain. But the dog turned at the entrance and stood at bay, defying her to come. "Pet!" Rose snarled at her. "Some pet!"

Another flash burnt the sky. More thunder. A crash of bushes. "Get over!" Rose snarled at her again, and brandished the knife. The dog retreated backwards, still at bay. Rose heaved herself into the hole.

Then she saw another problem. The men would see the hole, the great, gaping hole. She squirmed around and reached out. There was a branch caught among the stones just on her right. She put down the knife, knelt, and heaved at the branch. It was heavy and awkward. She grazed her knuckles. Another heave. It jammed across the entrance. That would have to do. At least the hole wouldn't look so perfect a den. She knelt there, as far into the den as she dared to go, listening to the bitch growling behind her, listening to the men outside ...gripping the knife...ready...

They had seen her footprints. They thought she had robbed their snare. And worse! They had seen the dog's prints beside hers. They thought that she had stolen the dog. She listened to them calling..."Gyp! Gyp!" They whistled. Would she answer them? Would she make a

noise and show them where she was? Rose dared not
breathe. The dog was quiet now. Absolutely silent. She
could almost feel her listening, almost feel her dreading
being found.

The men talked about her. Rose listened, right beside
them. Gyp was worth a fortune in skins, Gyp was, they
said. Just for her own sake she was worth a fortune,
but she was in whelp, too, and they could get ten skins
for every pup.

Thunder crashed, closer now. Rose heard the hard
thud of monstrous hail stones. The deluge had begun.
The men were worried. They were talking of a torrent.
What was a torrent? They said that they must go. They
ran. Rose breathed again as she heard them splashing
along the ditch, still whistling, still calling Gyp. She
began to marvel at the worth of a dog. A fortune in
wolf skins! And every pup worth ten! Pup. That was
a new word. For Baby dog say pup—and presumably
Mother dogs had more than one pup at a time.

Behind her she heard eager, squeaking whimperings
and the sound of a rough tongue licking, and then a
contented, gurgling sucking. The pups were feeding.
Suddenly Rose felt hungry.

She moved away from Gyp, and sat back, closer to
the entrance, her knees bent up to her chin, her shoulders
cramped against the curve of the drain. It wasn't a comfortable hiding place, but it was secret and it was safe.
I'm like Mole in his hole, she thought. I'm secret and
safe.

But the hole didn't stay safe. Rose huddled there in
the darkness, groping in the satchel for root cakes and
apples, listening to the deluge as it tore past overhead.
Rain and hail beat down with fury, but it would be a
sudden fury, sudden violence which soon passed. There

would be silence afterwards, a delicious, peaceful silence, to be valued and enjoyed before the Long Storm began.

But this time there was no silence. In the distance she could hear the roar of rushing water, a wave of rushing water. Torrent! That was what torrent meant. It was like in the book—a river flooding after rain.

Next moment the head-wave of the flash-flood roared past below her in the ditch. She heard stones rattling, crashing past. The force of it! She was above it. There's luck!

. But she wasn't above it. The great mass of water built up between the ditch walls. It began to wash into the drain. Undermined, the branch slid away and spun off at speed in the dark water. She would have to move out—fast! She retrieved the knife and pushed it into the satchel, and fumbled with the strap. The water was washing over her feet, soaking the seat of her tunic. Quick!

The dog was standing up, shaking off the pups. They whined piteously. So did she. Silly dog! A big mistake she had made, having babies in a hole that flooded. Serve her right if they all went...But how could she have known that the hole flooded? There hadn't been a Three Storm Group for months. She must never have seen the ditch full of water like this. Dogs *weren't* stupid, Grandmother said. This one simply hadn't known.

Rose crouched there, looking at her. She had picked up one pup, ready to carry it to safety. Three more squirmed around her feet, crying, as the water lapped at their round, warm bellies. Babies had to be looked after. Babies had to be saved. Grandmother's rule. She can't bite me with her mouth full. Rose flipped back the satchel flap, scooped up the pups, and stowed them in on top of the survival bag. The knife would have to go down deeper. Too bad if she needed it in a hurry. But she wouldn't. Nothing and no one would be out in a Three Storm Group.

The torrent tore at her legs as she crawled backwards out of the drain. She couldn't stand. It wrenched at the satchel and pulled the strap tight against her neck. She dragged herself back up on to the drain edge. She would have to climb up. So would the dog. This torrent could sweep a dog away like driftwood on the tide.

There was a root above her head. Rose gripped it with one hand, reaching upwards with the other. Beside her the dog scrabbled, trying to climb. Its claws scraped and scratched on the stone wall. It slipped and was pressed against Rose's legs by the force of the water. Rose reached down and grabbed it by the neck like Boss grabbed ferrets. It had loose skin there. Rose took a firm grip of a handful of skin and heaved. The dog struggled and scrabbled again—and disappeared over the top of the bank. Rose followed it.

"Now where?" she wondered.

The dog knew exactly where. She had a den in reserve. Another place to take her pups, just in case. Sensible dog! Now she set off, the one pup hanging limply from her jaws, and Rose followed her, hugging the other three in the sodden satchel.

8
The Cave

The dog carried her puppy to a cave. She followed a narrow, animal track straight through the dripping wood, and out into the open again. The strange, gray, mid-storm light softened all edges. Shapes merged with shapes. The squat structure which Rose had seen from the hummock seemed just a rise in the surface of Earth. Even when they passed close to it its sides looked blurred and rounded. Rose hardly noticed it.

But inside the squat hut a small, emaciated woman with a baby in her arms peered out through a crack in its turf-covered, stone walls and saw Rose. She moaned with fear and shrank back into the huddle of women and children who squatted or lay in the darkness there.

"What is it? What d'you see?" they whispered.

"Werewolf!" she said. "Upright, walking...saw its head, its ears."

"Aah..." they moaned and pressed closer to each other.

"Werewolf, werewolf..." The whisper spread. Around the hut it flew, and it reached the man they called Chief. "Werewolf, werewolf!" a young man told him.

"Crud!" Chief snarled at him. "Shut their faces." He watched, glaring at them all with contempt and hatred as the young men tried to beat the women into silence.

But they wouldn't be quiet. They were terrified, really terrified. One of them *had* seen something. And then even he, who had spent years inventing objects of terror

to use to frighten his small tribe and keep them in fear
of disobeying him, even he began to feel afraid.

But he knew that it wasn't a werewolf that that fool
woman had seen. Werewolves were only ideas on the
telly in the Old Days. His father had told him about
them. Good ideas, mind! Useful! But only ideas. All the
same, that woman had seen something. He would take
a look around when the wind had blown itself out. It
might be something to do with those footprints mixed
up with his bitch's tracks. Yeah, when the gale had
blown out he would take a look around.

Rose kept her eyes focused on the dog. She hurried after
her. Her one hope lay with that dog. The hope that
she had made a safer choice for her reserve den.

Just past the squat structure the path dropped sui-
cidally over the edge of a low cliff into a hole in the
ground. Bomb crater? Rose wondered. No, it was too
big for a bomb crater. And it was flat at the bottom.
There were paths down there too. It must be something
from the Old Days.

The dog scrambled down the steep path. Across the
level ground at the bottom she hurried, and up the other
side. There was a cave almost at the top of the cliff
on this side, a safe cave, safe from storm, rain, flood
and wind.

Rose couldn't understand why this cave hadn't been
the dog's *first* choice for her den. She knelt on the dry
floor beside her as she put down her puppy and asked
for Rose's three. Rose lifted them carefully from the
satchel and laid them gently beside the other one. They
were wet, but they were still warm. They squeaked and
lifted trembling heads towards their mother. The other
one didn't look too good, though. It looked as though it

wouldn't last. She put out her hand to feel if it was warm. Immediately the dog's hard, resisting snout jammed against her hand. She didn't snap this time. She didn't growl. But her eyes flashed warning.

Rose retreated to the other side of the cave. She was too tired to eat. All she wanted was sleep. She had to sleep in that bag from Grandfather's secret. Rules. Obediently she unfolded it and crept inside.

Much later she woke to thunder. Storm! For a moment she shrank into herself. Storm... The Voice... Wailing... Boss... Then she remembered what had happened. She sat up. Rain, like a gray curtain, hung and poured and lashed beyond the cave mouth. Water, nothing but water —and she was thirsty.

"Water, water everywhere, nor any drop to drink," Grandmother always said. Rose slid from the survival bag and looked for the satchel. She would reach out and stand her cup outside and leave it to fill. Where was that satchel?

A flash of lightning showed her the satchel. It lay, bundled roughly, against the wall of the cave. Apples were strewn everywhere. And the dog was cowering, curved protectively around her sleeping puppies, her eyes brave but full of apprehension.

Rose howled with rage. "You cheat! Cheat! Cheat! Cheat! *My* food! *My* food!" She saw the knife, gleaming, near her hand. She picked it up...

But no. This dog was a Mother. She needed food. Rose kicked an apple at her, hard, and put down the knife. "I never liked smoked rat bits anyway," she told her. "You're welcome to them. You could have left the cakes, though. P'raps you missed one." She picked up the satchel. A dead puppy lay hidden beneath it. "Aw... ahh... ahh... " Rose began to wail—then remembered.

Rules. No Boss. No wailing. "No Boss talk neither, and you made me do that too," she said to the dog.

The dog had begun to whine as soon as she saw the pup exposed. "No wailing!" Rose snarled at her. "I'll bury it right for you." She covered it with the satchel again as she looked around the cave for stones. There were plenty. Soon, she had a satisfactory cairn built over and around the pathetic, limp shape against the wall, satisfactory to both herself and Gyp.

They shared the cup of water, and Rose settled down to sort through her apples and nuts. She would have to be careful not to eat too much at once. This food had to last a week. Grandmother had said the walk would take a week. That was seven days, but one had gone already. How many were left?

Rose held up her left hand, fingers outstretched. That was only five. She needed another one. She stuck out her foot. That was six. She would make six piles and remember how many apples and nuts were in each pile and only eat that number.

The six heaps of food were disappointingly small, and Rose realized that she was going to feel very hungry every day. She would have to make a Rule, and *make* herself not eat even one more nut each day than she was allowed. She thought of the book and the food those animals had taken with them when they went walking, food which she had never tasted, but which Grandmother said was delicious but not worth tormenting yourself with thinking about it. She bit into a withered apple and put out the cup for more water. Water could feel quite filling, but it was a pity about those cakes. So pets cheated, eh. If only she had known she would have fastened the satchel tightly. She would take more care of her apples and nuts now, just in case. She pulled the

satchel towards her—and then she remembered Grandfather's picture. Where was Grandfather's picture? If
that dog had torn it up or lost it she *would* kill her...

Her panic and anger subsided again as she felt inside
the satchel and found that the picture was still inside it.
So was a scrap of smoked meat, which she decided to
keep to suck as she walked again when the storm was over.

She took out the picture carefully. It was wet and
badly creased, but she could still read "Jack Gibbs" on
the back of it, and she could still see the smooth, brown,
smiling face of the young man whom Grandmother had
picked, all that time ago When Things Were Going
Wrong. Rose liked Grandmother's stories of Grandfather. She knew them all. She made herself comfortable
in the survival bag and settled down to remember...

Jack had been clever, Grandmother said, clever and
as kind and gentle as a woman. Privately, Rose had
always thought that that was a stupid thing to say.
Women *weren't* kind and gentle. Only Joyce. Poor Joyce.
And Mother. But Eddie was kinder than Sharon and
Pat, and much more gentle than that awful Marilyn.
Perhaps it was a saying from the Old Days. It didn't
really matter.

All that mattered was that Grandfather hadn't been
like Boss or Boss's father. Grandfather had been a scientist and a poet in the Old Days. Scientists and poets
were wonderful, Grandmother said, and When Things
Went Wrong he had been made Leader. He had made
good Rules, Rules like: Everybody can go for walks and
look at the hill; Everybody must learn to read books;
Everybody must keep right away from the Hole and
not touch the box that makes the Voice. Grandfather
understood all about the Voice, Grandmother said. She
said that Video boxes like the one in the Hole had been

nice in the Old Days, when there had been *real* Telly. They had been interesting, like books. Nobody had wailed in the Old Days...and nobody would ever have wailed now if Grandfather hadn't been killed, and Leaders went out and Bosses came in.

Grandmother said that Boss's father, the first Boss, had been a good friend to Grandfather, but he wasn't clever, and he knew that he would never be as good a leader as Grandfather had been, and he knew that the other men, who were all gone now, would always be grumbling that he wasn't as good as Jack. So he didn't even try to be as good. Instead he changed all the Rules. He made all the Rules opposite to the ones Jack had made so that he could be quite different. Nobody was to walk out of Camp; Nobody was to go to look at that hill; Nobody was to read (he couldn't, so nobody else must).

He never went into the Hole. That was one thing in his favor, Grandmother said. It was his son, the Boss that Rose was afraid of, who had discovered that storms made the Voice come. It was this Boss who had begun the wailing, and made that Rule. Rose wasn't sure who had made the Rule about no singing. Her Boss, probably. He was always so miserable that hearing anybody singing would make him furious. But now he was gone and she could sing as much as she liked.

She sang now, as she sat in the cave, safe from the Storm, with Gyp contentedly nursing her pups. She sang the song that Grandfather had made up in the Old Days. Grandmother said that he had made it up about a flower called a rose, but he had always known that the words meant more than they seemed to say, that the song was not really about a flower at all, but about something much more important, though even he who had written it didn't know what the meaning could be. He had often wondered about it with his brother when he first wrote it down in the Old Days, and, After Things Went Wrong he wondered about it with Grandmother. "Why, for instance," he would wonder, "why did I think 'golden hound,' and not 'golden *hand*'? Golden hand would have made much more sense, but golden *hound* were the words that came to me, so golden hound it had to be," he had said.

When he first met Grandmother, whose name was Rosy, he had said that she could have the song for her own, for, perhaps, it had been about her all the time. And when Rose began to learn it Grandmother had said that she could share it. Rose sang it now.

Rose, sweet Rose, that comes in Winter,
To warm my heart and still my tears.
Come with your golden hound. Bring Summer
To this lone hill in these troubled years.

Golden hound! Rose thought sleepily. Fancy! Now *I've* got a golden hound. Grandmother had had a golden hound when Grandfather first met her. At least, Grandfather had called him a golden hound, because Grandfather was a poet. Grandmother always said he was just a big, yellow dog. Rose looked across the cave at Gyp and wondered if Grandmother would say that she was just a yellow dog. Probably, she thought. But I'm going to call her a golden hound. Pity I've got to walk on and leave her and those pups. Worth ten wolf skins each, fancy!

She wriggled down farther into the survival bag and, thinking of the fortune in skins...and Mr. Toad's fortune in the book...and how comfortable Toad Hall was because of his fortune, and of all the food Mr. Toad had... and everything else...because of...fortune...she fell asleep again.

9
Why Gyp is Worth a Fortune

Rose woke to the howling of the day of gales. She sat up in the warm bag and looked out. And immediately she saw why the cave had not been Gyp's *first* choice as a den. The mid-storm light was now all blown away, so was the curtain of gray rain. Now Rose could see clearly the squat structure which she had passed so closely. She shivered as she remembered just how closely ...She could see, now, that it was a hut.

People lived in huts. There would be people in that one. People who were worse than Boss, Grandmother said. And they were just on the other side of this huge hole.

She sat all day, watching the hut, watching and worrying. She must get out of this cave. As soon as the wind blew itself away she must get out. But not in daylight or she would be seen. She would have to escape at night and walk at night until she was far away from this place—at night, when wolves prowled.

Her mother had been killed by wolves. You always went the way your mother went, Grandmother said. Rose switched her thoughts away quickly.

The hill! She would think about the hill. She mustn't walk unless she could *see* the hill. Rules. But she wouldn't be able to see the hill in the dark! A light! Grandmother had said there had been a light on the hill at night. Was there still a light? There *must* be a light.

She shared her last cup of water with Gyp. Afterwards they were both still thirsty.

There was a pool on the flat ground at the bottom of the quarry, which was what the huge hole had been in the Old Days. Gyp came and sat beside Rose and they both looked at the pool and licked their lips. Gyp leant against her. She felt almost like Grandmother did, leaning there...almost. Rose put her arm around her and thought of Grandmother. She hoped that Grandmother had enough food. She hoped that Baby wouldn't cry without his mother. She hoped that they would both keep warm.

She hugged Gyp, and the dog arched her graceful neck and licked the hand that rested on her shoulder. She licked it carefully and thoroughly, between each finger and around the thumb, nibbling gently at the nails.

Rose sighed with pleasure, and marvelled. Her hand was as clean as one of the pups. She stroked Gyp's coarse, warm hair with her other hand, and felt the silky softness of her fine, black ears—and then she saw a flea. Aw, fleas! Rose loved catching fleas. She caught this one and cracked it between her nails, and then looked for more. She caught fleas like this for Grandmother. Pets were nice, she decided. She began to think that it was a terrible shame that she had to walk on and leave this one.

Late in the afternoon, when the wind was less strong, Gyp could bear her thirst no longer. The pups were whimpering. Her milk was drying up. She must drink.

Rose watched her as she slunk down the side of the old quarry, pressing herself low among the stones and scrub bushes. Gyp had done this sort of thing before. Rose envied her as she watched her drink. She licked her lips. She was parched.

Suddenly, she saw a movement. A rat! No! Something else. Small. Furry. White-tailed. A rabbit! A rabbit like in the book! Gyp was after it. Aw! Could she run! *That* was why she was worth a fortune. Rose understood at once. Gyp could hunt... "Got it!" she said, with satisfaction.

Gyp brought the rabbit back to the cave and laid it at Rose's feet. Her eyes were bright, her tail wagging at the tip. She was eager and pleased.

"Good!" Rose told her. "Good pet! But you eat it. I like cooked meat best. I've got to be hungrier than this to eat meat raw."

She wished, later, as she watched the dog lying full and satisfied, feeding her pups again, that she had taken a leg of the rabbit. She was hungry enough now to eat it raw. She broke her Rule and helped herself to one of tomorrow's apples, and waited for nightfall.

She began to worry about breaking the Rule, about whether her food would be enough for the rest of the week, about how few days she had left in the week. All this waiting! Tonight she must walk enough for two days or her food, and Grandmother's and Baby's, would be all gone long before she reached the hill. And Grandmother and Baby had to make theirs do until she came back again.

Well, there was nothing she could do about their food except hurry, and if she was going to have to hurry she was going to have to find more to eat for herself. She began to look at Gyp speculatively, and then she began to plan.

If she could get this dog to come with her, there would be no shortage of food, as long as they could see things to catch. And it would be stupid to leave her behind if she was worth a fortune. The pups too, they were worth ten wolf skins each. Rose spread out all her fingers.

That was ten. A lot of wolfskins! Not that she and Grandmother and Baby needed wolfskins. It was *help* they
needed. She had to bring back help, Grandmother said.
That was a thought. What did Grandmother mean by
help? Did she mean food? Or somebody to look after
them? Or what...?

Grandmother seemed to be sure that the people who
lived on the hill were not like Boss. What were they like,
then? Were they like Grandfather? Were they all scientists
and poets on the hill? Rose considered it all as the light of
the day of gales faded, and she decided that Gyp and her
pups were going to come with her. Gyp liked her now.
Gyp seemed to have decided that she was *her* pet now.
She would keep Gyp and take her back to Camp with
her. But the pups she would exchange for food and whatever sort of help the people on the hill would give her.

In the book the animals had had money to buy food
and things they needed. People had had money to use
like that in the Old Days, Grandmother said. It would
be worth trying to use the pups like money. She could
carry them to the hill in the satchel. But how was she
going to persuade Gyp to let her put the pups in the
satchel? She hadn't snapped at her for two days now. All
the same, she would have to make absolutely sure that
she couldn't snap before she tried to touch them.

She decided to tempt Gyp with the last piece of rat
meat, to get her away from them, or at least keep her
busy eating while she picked them up. Once they were
in the satchel and the satchel slung over her shoulder,
Gyp would follow her anywhere.

The plan worked. Rose didn't wait until nightfall. She
decided that nobody would come out of that hut so late in
the day. Nobody sensible ever came out so near nightfall,
unless, like herself, they had to. Wolves came out at

night. People stayed in. If anybody should see her and Gyp they wouldn't come out now. And if they did come after her tomorrow, well, she would be far away by then.

As Gyp chewed the revolting morsel of meat, Rose quickly stowed the puppies inside the satchel. She laid them on top of the survival bag which she had folded carefully so that, if they did wet, her apples and the inside of the bag would stay dry. The knife she would carry.

With Gyp whining gently and leaping at the satchel, she climbed out of the quarry and crouched for a moment on the edge of the cliff, looking back. There was no movement near the squat hut. No one was watching, as far as she could tell. She looked beyond it to the wood — and then she looked beyond the wood.

And she could see the pine tree, stark and solitary on the hummock. Behind it a cluster of rusty towers and ruins stood out, bleak, against the cold, gray sea... Camp...Grandmother...Baby..."Aw...aah...No! No wailing." She turned her back on it and scrambled away, still crouching low. She mustn't stand up on the skyline. She mustn't stand up until she was hidden from that hut.

She reached a clump of gorse, and then stood up. And, immediately, she saw the hill. It stood, straight in front of her, far away across the plain. The freezing mist had gone, blown away for a few days by storm and gale. She could see a river. There were trees! There were hedges and ruins stretching away as far as she could see, and all of them leading, pointing, it seemed, to the hill.

And from the highest point of the tower that stood on the summit of the hill, shone a bright light. It was a steady, beaming light. The only light on Earth, just as Grandmother had said.

10
Wolves

Rose, with Gyp close at her heels, marched towards that light. What a light it was! So bright! Anyone who made that light must be a scientist. A scientist! Fancy! She must be going to meet a scientist. Rose knew all about scientists. Grandmother had told her...Scientists were clever. *They* understood all about the Video box that made the Voice. *They* knew why the rain had suddenly turned yellow, back When Things Went Wrong. *They* knew why Earth had quaked all over, why rivers had run *away* from the sea, why the sea had swept over the land. *They* knew why the moon was hidden now. *They* knew why the sun, whose light, Grandmother said, had once been so bright that you couldn't look at it, and so warm that you felt as though you were sitting by the fire, *they* knew why the sun now drifted like a silver ghost above the white sky which was not really sky, Grandmother said, but whirling cloud. Always cloud, even when the storms came down below them, always cloud, and cold...

They knew why the snow had fallen When Things Went Wrong, they knew about the ice on the sea and the freezing mist that still lingered even now, the hail stones as big as Baby's fist, and the brilliant, flashing light that filled the sky at night sometimes, but should have stayed far off in the North, Grandmother said, like the wind, the bitter wind that made her Thritis hurt, and took away the food she used to have and made her so hungry, Grandmother said, that sometimes she wished that there had been the Bomb instead of Everything Going Wrong. "It would be better for our Earth to be gone, than to be left with us living here on her like this," Grandmother said, when she was hungry and her Thritis hurt and Boss was being Boss.

But "*Scientists* would put it all right," Grandmother said, when she felt better. *Scientists* would make the grass grow thick upon Earth again. *They* would make leaves grow on all the trees. *They* would make places where you could be always warm, and grow *big* apples... and *scientists* would make Babies always *last*...

Maybe that was the sort of help she had to ask for, Rose thought. Someone to come back with her and help them make Baby last. She marched on towards the light, singing quietly.

They first heard the wolves as the last purple streak of sunset faded into blackness low on the horizon behind them. Rose felt Gyp press against her legs. "It's all right," she told her. "They're miles away. They're only calling to each other, saying whose patch is whose."

But the next howl was closer. Was it still just a call? She wasn't sure. The next one was closer still. And this one was not a call. It was the "start hunting" howl. The howl meant that they had found their prey, their It.

"We might not be It." Rose kicked Gyp away from her legs. Gyp was trembling now. Rose began to jog along, holding the satchel to stop it bumping against her side. Gyp whimpered.

Another howl! Short...excited...uncontrollable... And close! Rose couldn't pretend any more. She and Gyp *were* It. She ran.

Wolves were starving, Boss said. No rats on the plain

now, Boss said. Wolves had eaten all rats. Wolves were starving now...

She had to find a ruin, a hut. No! No huts. No Bosses. A cave. Where? No cave there. A hedge. There were holes in hedges, big, scraped-out holes, or thick gorse and boulders...

She had the knife. If you cut a wolf the pack would make that It instead of you, Boss said.

Wolves were mad, Boss said. Don't let them bite you or you go mad too, Boss said. Boss knew about wolves.

Rose ran, trying to remember the view she had seen from above the cave. Where had there been a hedge? Where...where? She couldn't see a hedge. She turned to left and right, peering. Everything was shadows. Shadows that reached towards her, shadows cast by the light on the hill. Another short, ecstatic howl. Closer! Shadows everywhere...

A row of trees loomed up on her right. They caught the hill light in their branches. Rose swerved and turned towards them, tripped over Gyp, stumbled, ran stumbling...Trees! She could climb trees. Wolves couldn't. But nor could Gyp! She couldn't leave Gyp, the Mother, her pet. She couldn't leave Gyp. But she'd have to. No! She couldn't! She'd have to...aah...But *look!*

Among the trees, a large-boled, ancient oak, limbless, lumpy, sat dead and hollow. Hollow tree like in the book ...Mole...The Terror...

Rose was through the crack in the trunk at once. No hesitation! Gyp tangled with her legs. She tripped again, began to fall forward into the darkness, twisted, and fell back...

Wolf! Rose saw white fangs, red eyes above her, felt her wolfskin snatched from her shoulder. She slashed out with the knife, screaming, heard a howl of pain...

And then, oh, the snarling, the fighting, the stench of blood, and the howling of a hunt come to a satisfying conclusion.

The pack settled down, where Rose could still hear it all, to gorge itself on its own leader. Boss had known. Wolves *were* mad since Everything Went Wrong. Boss had said they were. Boss had been right.

But then Rose had a terrifying thought. Had that wolf bitten her? "Aw...aah..." No! No wailing! But a scratch would be enough, Boss said. Rose felt her shoulder beneath the tunic, and ran her fingertips minutely over every square centimeter of her arm. She prodded a bruise, an old one. One Marilyn had given her. She found a scratch! But it had a scab. The scratch was old, too. She was safe from wolf madness. Luck! Only her wolf-skin cloak torn at the shoulder. Real luck!

But the pups were crying. Had she fallen on them? Were they crushed? Would crushed pups still be worth ten skins each? Were there still three? She groped around in the satchel...One...two...three...They had all lasted! She handed them over to Gyp, who settled down to clean and feed them.

Then she knelt, watching the moving shadows, the dark, red-eyed, white-fanged, snarling shadows that prowled in and out among the black trunks of the trees. She was cold. Freezing! Good! She wouldn't fall asleep if she was cold. She would just wrap the bag around her tonight, to make sure she didn't really freeze, then she would stay awake, stay awake and watching, with the knife ready.

The wolves didn't attack again, but they didn't go away either. They too stayed watching until the white light of dawn exposed them for the pitiful, sick creatures that they had become since Things Went Wrong. Then they went to hide. And Rose sank, exhausted, against Gyp's back, and dreamt that she was in the hut with Grandmother.

11
Willow Trees

Rose dreamed that Baby was crying. Then she woke, and it was the pups who were crying, wobbling their blind heads up at Gyp, as she stood over her with a newly-killed rabbit in her jaws. It was going to be a good day, Rose knew it. And it was.

The sky curved above her like a great, silver bowl. The clear air seemed to tingle, sharp with frost. To her right, immediately beside the trees, a river, full to over-flowing, rolled turgidly towards the sea. It came from the hill. She had seen it yesterday from the higher ground. She shielded her eyes from the glare of the sky and gazed east.

How ever far had she run last night? Or was it a trick of the light? The hill looked so close! It seemed no more than a morning's walk away. But it was probably a trick of the light. Grandmother said that light was always playing tricks since Everything Went Wrong. But, suddenly, it didn't matter how far away or how close the hill was. It was within reach. She would just keep walking until she arrived there.

She shared this rabbit with Gyp. Gyp ate most of it. Rose didn't enjoy raw meat. It was so tough and bloody.

In the book the animals had carried things to light fires with everywhere they went. Grandmother had told her about those things. All they were, were tiny splinters of wood dipped in something which flared into a flame the moment they rubbed it against the box they kept them in. "Matches!" Rose said. "A box of matches, fancy! Cooked food anywhere you happened to be, not just in the hut." She wished that she had a box of matches as she tore at the tough leg of rabbit with her teeth and chewed at the meat until her jaws ached.

When she had eaten as much as she could, they both drank from the river, taking care to keep out of reach of the terrible snatching current. Then Rose lifted the sleeping pups into the satchel, threw a stone happily at a crow that had flown down to scavenge, and set out, the knife once again in her hand. Wolves didn't prowl in daylight. But Bosses did.

The hill seemed just as close, but also just as far away when Rose stopped to eat an apple and let Gyp feed the pups, but still the distance didn't matter at all. The walk that morning had been wonderful.

Soon after they left the hollow tree they had found grass. *Thick* grass! Gyp had rolled in it ecstatically, just like Mole had in the book, and Rose had rolled too, and pressed her face into it to see what it felt like. It smelled good enough to eat, but when she tried, it formed a matted ball in her mouth which was difficult to swallow. They had walked on grass all morning.

Now, from where she sat, she could see grass stretching away into the distance on both banks of the river. *Green* grass! *Green* Earth, not brown and yellow Earth like when she was at Camp, but green. Fancy! *Green* Earth!

And from here the hill looked green. Could the hill actually be covered all over with grass? Grandmother had told her about green hills, but she hadn't known that they were green because of grass. Rose shaded her eyes to look at the hill again. It was then that she saw the willow trees.

She knew that they were willow trees because there was a picture of them in the book. And now she was going to see a real one. She was going to see a real willow tree, to *feel* a real willow tree. She could hardly believe it. And suddenly it was important, terribly important. Rose was terrified that if she waited, if she didn't hurry to them right away, the willow trees wouldn't be there when she reached the place where she could see them, that they would prove to be not real at all.

Hastily, she eased the pups away from the warm cradle of Gyp's flank, and put them into the satchel. How they were growing! They were taking up twice as much room as they had the day before yesterday. And Gyp didn't mind her taking them now. Gyp thought that putting pups into the satchel was Rules. Rose's Rules! Everything was suddenly wonderful. Rose ran towards the willows.

And they *were* real willows, though there was no wind in their branches. But then, there wouldn't be, not until it was nearly time for the next storm. And they had no leaves, of course, just branches. But beautiful branches, golden and slender, curving with delicate grace to dip into the fast-flowing flood. The river seemed to want to pull these willows from the bank and take them with it. And no wonder! Who wouldn't want to take a willow tree everywhere they went if they could.

Rose walked beside them, stopping at each one to feel its bark, half expecting to see Mole or Toad or Badger ...and Ratty too, now, because, here, beside the willows, she knew that Grandmother had been right when she said that the Water Rat wasn't like the loathsome rats she knew at Camp. At last Rose was happy about Ratty.

Now Grandmother's book was perfect...and what if she and Gyp should find the island where Mole and Ratty had found their wonderful lord with the pipes that made magic music? What had Grandmother called them? The Pipes of Pan! That was it! Grandmother had a song about them too, as well as the writing in her book. "Come follow, follow, follow," it began. Mole and Ratty had followed, and they had found the lost Baby otter. Rose wandered along all day, dreaming and singing...

Rose, sweet Rose, that comes in Winter
To warm my heart and still my tears.
Come with your golden hound. Bring Summer
To this lone hill in these troubled years.

At about the time that Rose found the willow trees, a man with a black wolf-dog at his heels climbed the side of the quarry and stepped into the cave. Rabbit fur! The bitch had been here...Where was she now?

The dog sniffed at a pile of stones, and whined. Somebody built that. Chief kicked at the cairn. Dead pup! So she had had her pups. Somebody had her *and* her pups...*his* bitch, *his* pups! He swore to himself.

The wolf-dog tore up the dead pup and ate it, then followed Chief to the top of the quarry side. They both stood there, gazing out across the plain.

Gyp's coat gleamed like a streak of pale flame as she sped from the trees behind another rabbit. They saw her instantly. Hunting! My bitch...and she's got it. Of course she's got it! he thought bitterly, and spat into the mud. Who's taken her?

He watched the trees closely, and saw Rose as she stepped out to take the rabbit that Gyp brought straight back to her. For one terrible moment Chief was afraid.

It *was* a werewolf! That fool woman had been right. It was a werewolf, all covered in fur, walking upright. He cringed for a moment, and almost slunk back to his hut. Then his brute common sense came back. It couldn't be a werewolf!

He watched again, carefully. He saw Rose stoop to pat and stroke the hound. He saw the satchel swing forward from her shoulder as she stooped. He saw her twist her body to swing it back into place again, and then turn away from Gyp and step out again towards the hill.

A boy! he thought. Small...thin...sneaking off with my bitch. Doubtless a boy from that blasted hill. He saw Gyp leaping at the satchel eagerly. He knew that movement. She wants her pups. *My* pups...in that bag.

He looked at the sky. He couldn't go after them now. Night would be upon him before he got back to the hut if he went now. Night and its wolves. But that boy was on his own and walking. That boy wouldn't get back to the hill before night came. He would have to shelter and hide from night, too. Even people from the hill had to do that. He would still be on the plain in the morning. Off *my* patch...but so what! It'll be worth the risk to get back that bitch and the pups.

Chief made up his mind. He would follow that boy early next morning—and he would *get* him.

12
So Near...

Rose slept among the willow trees. She had noticed, as she walked beside them, that, every now and then, one of them had fallen and lay, decaying gently, covered with a creeping plant with shiny, dark-green leaves. She had stopped to feel those wonderful leaves, and had found a hollow place scraped out beneath the tree, dry and quite hidden by the thick, green curtain of the plant. Some animal must have scraped out the soil. She couldn't even guess which animal it could have been. It worried her, but Gyp hadn't worried. Gyp had approved of it, and had looked expectantly at the satchel. "Not yet," Rose had told her. She walked on towards the hill, until she found a hollow at the time when she judged night to be too near to risk walking in the hope of finding another one even further on.

They shared the afternoon rabbit, as they had shared the morning one, and then, when Rose spread out the survival bag on the dry floor of the hollow, Gyp pushed the pups on to the edge of it, and settled down, her back curved against the crook of Rose's knees. "Pet," Rose said to her, and fondled her soft, warm ears.

Pets' ears were something Grandmother hadn't mentioned, though Rose felt sure that Grandmother must have known about them. I'm going to take Gyp back with me, she thought. I'm going to take her back as well as the help from the hill, and then Grandmother will have a chance to enjoy pets' ears again. And I'll tell her I saw willow trees, like she did in the Old Days. Rose lay, thinking about Grandmother. Grandmother would have liked to see these willow trees. It was a pity she couldn't. But she would tell her exactly how they looked.

She parted the ivy curtain. There was the light, beaming out at her from the hill. The hill, where she would find help, tomorrow, maybe, or the day after tomorrow...

Rose woke early with the first light, and lay watching the pups knead their front paws against Gyp's soft side as they gorged themselves on her milk. "Feed, sleep and be carried to the hill, that's all you do. Fff!" she said to them, and then slid from the bag, careful not to disturb them. But what? Something was wrong! What...Gyp's whole body had suddenly tensed. Rose stared at her. Why? What was it?

She felt, rather than saw the movement just outside the hollow. Wolves, like before! The knife! Instantly she snatched it up, arched across Gyp, rolled over, looked up...*Black* wolf!

With all the strength of her thin, hard body, Rose struck upwards at the throat of the great, black head that thrust, like magic, through the curtain of leaves. Blood gushed. The wolf-dog fell, gurgling, on top of her. She heaved it off, bending her legs beneath it, kicking, pushing with her one free arm. The knife pulled out cleanly as the carcass fell away. More blood! The carcass twitched.

Rose stared at it, her mouth grimacing, wide, down-turned, mask-like. It was not a wolf. It was a dog. A pet. Somebody's pet. A *man's* pet. A man who would come after her...

She must run. She must pack the pups. She reached

for the satchel and grasped the survival bag, pulling
at it, sweeping the pups and Gyp from it into the recesses
of the hollow. Now! Into the satchel with the bag. Quick!
Quick! She scrambled, crawling backwards, from the
hollow.

And then she was aware of Gyp again. Gyp, who
had been standing shivering and whining as she watched
her, was now cringing in complete silence, arched protectively over the heap of supine pups.

Rose whirled around and crouched, the satchel pressed
against her body, the knife held ready.

Chief stood at some distance. He hadn't seen Rose
kill his dog. But now he saw its carcass. Now he saw
the knife. He saw the satchel. And then he looked at
Rose. A *girl!* For a moment his eyes glinted dangerously.
Then the look in them hardened again. He squared his
shoulders and flexed the muscles in his arms. "My pups!"
he said, and held out one thick-fingered hand, palm
uppermost.

"No!" Rose spat at him.

He snorted like an angry bull, and stepped towards
her. She brandished the knife. And then he leered at
her, his eyes bright and cunning. Slowly, still watching
her carefully, he bent at the knee and reached out for
a stick.

A fight! A fight with a Boss. No! He'd make her gone!
She couldn't last against a Boss. "Aah!" The sound Rose
made was more a wail than a scream. "Aah!" She turned
and ran. He could have his pups, his Gyp. Aw...ah...
ah...*Her* Gyp! She wailed within herself. *Her* Gyp! But
still she ran.

She knew all about running. She had learned to run
when she was very young. Her Mother had been got
by wolves. *She* would be got like her Mother one day,

but not while she could run. And she would run safe from this Boss man. *He* wouldn't get her. He wouldn't want to, now that she had given up what was his.

She glanced back. He was coming! He was running after her. He was still coming. Why didn't he take his pups and let her go? She had left him his pups.

Rose ran. She sped like a deer across the grass of the plain. And Chief ran too, senseless at being defied by this girl, senseless with fury. He hadn't looked in the hollow beneath the fallen tree. He had simply seen the satchel which he had convinced himself, yesterday, held his pups. Now, senselessly, he was still convinced that they were there, that Rose was running away with his fortune in that satchel.

She could run! She'd got speed! But she wouldn't keep it up, not speed like that. She would slow down. He had chased like this before. He settled to a steady, rhythmic pace, a pace which he knew he could keep up for hours if necessary. But it wouldn't take hours. She would soon slow down.

He was right. All too soon, Rose felt the gap between them growing less...heard him coming closer...knew that he would get her. And the hill looked so near... the hill and help...Ah...aah...She *could* get there. She *must* get there. But he was closer...closer...closer... And the hill had been so near...

She felt his hand grab at her cloak and slip off it. She tried to leap sideways...to dodge...She leapt forward again...felt him grab again...

And then, suddenly, she was falling. The ground went, disappeared. Briefly she feared it was a cliff, another quarry. She screamed...looked down...and saw an animal, close, right beneath her. She screamed again as she recognized it. "Bear!"

Rose twisted in midair. The knife flew from her hand ...And, as she felt the hard floor of the deep ditch thud against her, and blackness closed in around her, she heard Chief screaming as he, too, fell.

13
Hill People

Gyp was barking, far away. I haven't gone this time, then. Blackness again.

Gyp was barking, close now. I still haven't gone! Mist. There was mist in her eyes. Rose screwed them shut. Aw! Her head hurt. Her head hurt the way it had when Boss had knocked her out for saying she wouldn't go into The Hole...Boss! She remembered the man like Boss. Where was he?

She raised her head a little, carefully, slowly. After knocking out, move with care and slowness. Rules! Careful now! She turned her head. The Boss man lay some distance from her—what was left of him. Blood! She was sick of blood. She lay back silently, closing her eyes against the glare of the silver sky.

And then Gyp was there, leaping and squirming, wriggling, darting forward to lick her face, darting back again. Then lying, hard and protective, upon her chest, growling. Someone else was there!

Instantly, like an animal, Rose was wide awake. Cautiously, eyes open and seeing now, she turned her head and looked where Gyp was looking.

It was a boy, a boy like Rory. A boy! He held two dead rabbits, tied together by their legs, hanging from one hand. And he held her knife in the other. Rose moved her hand until she felt a stone. Her fingers closed around it. Then she lay, stiff and tense, watching him...aware, in spite of her fear, that his clothes were not made of skins, that he was as clean as Gyp's three pups, and that he was afraid of her. He wasn't coming close. And why was he staring at Gyp? Was he afraid of Gyp? No, but he was staring at her...Aw! He couldn't have seen a dog before. He was like she was before she found Gyp. He had never seen a dog before.

But the boy had seen a dog before. He knew about dogs. Rose could tell that he did as soon as he spoke. "The golden hound," he said. "The golden hound!...Is she yours?"

"My pet!" Rose said possessively, trying to sound fierce.

"The golden hound," he said again, as though he couldn't believe what he was saying. "But where's the rose?" he asked.

Rose stared at him. He knew her song...but not properly. He didn't know *all* about it. "Stupid boy!" she said. "*I'm* Rose."

He stared at *her* then. "*You* are Rose...Rose is a *name*. The song is about a *girl* called Rose with a golden hound ...Oh!" He smiled at her happily. "Gibbs will believe *that*," he said, and then he ran away from her, calling, "Martyn, Martyn!"

He wasn't so stupid then. He had soon understood. But she must get him. This was her chance. Now! While he was turned away. Get him! She jerked herself upright, the stone between her fingers...Aah! Pain and blackness came again.

This time when the blackness cleared, Rose found herself looking up at a man, a Boss man, bending over her, and Gyp was barking at a distance. Gyp wasn't there to keep him off. Rose stared up at him, too terrified to move. And then she saw that he wasn't really like Boss. He did have hair on his lip and on his cheeks,

but his chin was bare and smooth and clean. And his
eyes…what were his eyes like? Not like Boss's eyes
at all. Not like a scientist's either, not like Grandfather's
in the picture. But like something she knew. Vaguely
she recalled the long-ago-eaten cow. Yes! The cow hadn't
just been hairy, horned and with a kick. The cow had
been a gentle creature. The cow had had brown eyes,
just like this man's. This man wouldn't hurt her.

"Rose?" he said. "Are you really called Rose?"

"Um," she grunted. So he knew the song too! A *man*
knew a song!

"Rose, sweet Rose," he said, "that doesn't smell so
sweet." He wrinkled his nose as he lifted her up in his
arms, and chuckled to himself.

Gyp began to bark again.

"The golden hound, the golden hound! She's not coming with us." The boy was there too. He began to pull
at Martyn's arm frantically. "She must come," he said,
"or it won't be complete."

"She's got pups." Rose looked down at him. "Baby
dogs. Mothers don't leave Babies. Rules."

"Pups!" The boy was overjoyed. "Golden pups?"

"*My* pups!" Rose snarled at him.

"All right, all right, *your* pups. But where?"

Rose had to trust him. She told him where to find
them. "There's my satchel somewhere. Take my satchel."
She gave her orders. "Gyp thinks 'Pups go in satchel'
is Rules now. She'll let you bring them in my satchel."

"Can I go, Martyn? Can I go and get them?" the boy
begged.

"Not on your own," Martyn said. "Get Thomas to
take you on Duke."

The boy ran ahead, calling to Thomas, as Martyn
began to walk along, carrying Rose, and soon, through

new, rapidly-descending darkness, Rose was aware that
he had passed her again, riding on a monstrous animal,
rather like the cow, with another man who had stopped
to look down at her for a moment, with gentle wonder.
Then she was being lifted on to something like a bed
on wheels, with another of the monstrous animals fixed
to it with poles and ropes. She recognized it. A horse
and cart...like in the book.

When the darkness cleared again, the cart was moving,
quite quickly, and it wasn't level any more, it was tilted.
Rose knew where she must be. She was on the hill,
climbing up the hill in a horse and cart. Wait till Grandmother heard this! She moved her head a little and looked
around. The tower rose above her, pointing at the sky.
And there were huts too. Huge huts! And another, thin,
tower, with arms that turned slowly in the gentle breeze.

The next time the blackness cleared, someone was
stripping her of her wolf skins. Rose grabbed at the
hand she could feel close to her neck even before she
could see it, and snarled and tried to bite it.

"Now, now!" It was an old woman's voice. Rose lay
still. "That's better! You wouldn't want to bite an old
grandmother, would you?" asked the voice. "Though,
by the look of you, poor, skinny, little mite that you
are, you'd be glad to bite into anything you could set
your teeth into."

Rose focussed on the voice and found the face. Was
this a Grandmother? This little, round woman? She
watched her, and obeyed meekly, as she tore off the
last wolf skin and began to wash her. It felt...how did
it feel? Better than sitting by the fire. So warm! And
what was that smell? It was so sweet you could eat it
without chewing.

"Tt, tt! That's a nasty bump," the old woman said

as she lathered Rose's hair. "Fell into our outer moat, didn't you? Martyn said you must have. Lucky you were that that bear didn't get you." She hesitated, and then went on kindly. "You know it got your poor father, poor little Rose."

What was that? Father? *Her* father?...Memory flooded back. "That Boss man was not my father," Rose snarled at her, annoyed that she could even think such a thing.

"Eh? Not your father? Who was he then? Surely not your husband?"

Rose didn't know that word, but she shook her head. That Boss man was *nothing* of hers. "He was nothing of mine," she told her.

"Eh?" The old woman shook her head. "My word, you do have a funny way of saying things. Don't you talk to each other, out there in the Camps?"

She dried Rose tenderly, and then dressed her in something which felt more soft and warm than even Baby's softest skins. Baby! Rose remembered why she had come there. "Help!" she said to the old woman. "I came for help."

The old woman sat down beside her on the couch where she lay, and held her hand. "*You* came for help?" she said. "Who in their right minds would tell a waif like you to get out of those Camps and cross that terrible plain to come to us for help?"

Rose looked up at her. She could trust her. She was a Grandmother. You could always trust a Grandmother. She decided to tell her...and she did. She told her how terrible the walk had been, about finding Gyp, about the flood, about the cave and the other hut, about the wolves and the man like Boss, and she told her why she had come, she told her about Grandmother and Baby, left waiting there in Camp.

The Grandmother listened...and she cried. Rose couldn't understand the crying. Only Mothers cried when Babies went. She couldn't understand it.

Someone knocked on the door while the old woman was crying. That was something else new. Knocking on the door...and it meant asking to come in. Rose raised her head and looked at the people who walked into the room when the old woman called to them.

They had brought Gyp. Gyp hurled herself on top of Rose, darting, licking, turning circles in delight. Rose laughed and held her still. The boy was there, with her pups. And what was that he had them in? She looked at the basket with admiration. Now that was a useful thing! He had made it out of twigs, by the look of it, or someone had. And what a good skin he had put in it to make the pups comfortable! He must know all about pets, just like Grandmother. She looked at the boy with interest.

And then more people came. And these people were definitely scientists. She knew it because they reminded her of Grandfather. Scientists at last! Two scientists and a Mother...that boy's Mother.

"This is Rose, Mother," the boy said, and the woman knelt beside Rose and she too cried.

I *am* going! That's what it is! Rose shrank back into the bed in fear. I'm going. They're crying because I'm not going to last any longer...But, no, that wasn't the reason.

"Rose, we'll soon have you as big and strong as Jacob here, and you and your golden hound can stay with us forever," the woman told her.

So she wasn't going! Rose relaxed again. And what a good thought that was, to stay with them forever — much more comfortable than Camp. Perhaps that was the help Grandmother meant. "I came for help," she told her.

"What?"

The old woman explained. "She came all that way on her own for help. She's left her grandmother and a baby in The Camps," she said, and then she told them everything that Rose had told her.

"We'll have to fetch them. They'll never survive out there. How long ago did she leave them? We'll have to go right away," the woman said.

But then one of the men spoke. Quietly and sadly he said, "We *should* go and fetch them, right away, Anne. I quite agree with you. But will our dear leader agree to it? Will this sweet Rose with her golden hound bring enough warmth to that cold, scientific heart to make Gibbs let us go?"

14
Gibbs

While Rose drank broth the like of which she had never tasted before, and ate biscuits which crumbled in her mouth, and Gyp's, Jacob's mother and father went to tell Gibbs about her. Rose was interested in the name. Gibbs...one of Grandfather's names.

The sad man stayed with her and the old woman and Jacob, and it seemed to Rose that he watched her constantly in much the same sort of way that she watched Gyp and her pups. She didn't like being watched like that. Nor did she like being talked about as though she couldn't talk herself. And that was what the man did next. He began to talk about her with the old woman.

"If this one is anything to go by, Camp children are stronger and more resilient than children on the hill," he said. "One of our children would have been flat on its back and complaining bitterly after a bump on the head like that."

"None of our children would have survived the plain long enough to have got as far as falling into our moat and getting the bump on its head," the old woman told him. "It hasn't spoiled your appetite either, has it, sweet Rose," she said, trying to draw Rose into the conversation. "Have a little drop more, eh? Just a little...and another barley cake. And don't waste this one on the hound. Jacob'll feed her. Tt, tt," she said, as Rose still insisted on sharing the biscuit with Gyp.

"I thought Camp children ate ravenously, like wolves,"

the man said. Rose began to feel annoyed with him.

"I don't know how you can bear to give any of it away." He spoke to her at last. "It must be the first real meal you've eaten for days."

Rose was inclined to think that it was the first real meal that she had ever eaten, but she wasn't going to admit that to him. Who did he think he was to talk about her as if she couldn't talk herself! She was appalled at his ignorance, too. He didn't even know the Rules about Mothers! "Gyp is a Mother," she explained to him, in the way Grandmother explained things she didn't understand to her. "Mothers are special. You feed Mothers extra, then their Babies will last, perhaps. Rules," she told him, and then added, "And pups are worth ten wolf skins each. The Boss man who chased me said. And that makes them worth looking after. *And* they're pets. You take care of pets and pets take care of you," she explained.

The man laughed. "I see what you mean," he said. "It's all common sense and reason, isn't it. My word! Common sense and reason in a Camp child! You're a good deal brighter than all the other Camp people I've seen, Rose," he said.

Rose resented the condescension in his voice. Who did he think he was! "My grandfather was a scientist," she told him, and would have said a lot more, but, suddenly, he had changed. Suddenly he was eager to know more, eager to talk to her.

"Your grandfather...a scientist," he said. "You've heard about scientists? What do you know about scientists?"

"Grandfather was a scientist," she repeated. What else did she know? "You are scientists on the hill. Grandmother told me about scientists."

He leaned forward earnestly. "What did your grandmother tell you about your grandfather? Did she tell you his name, perhaps?"

"It was Jack," she said, and sang the poem.

Jack and Jill went up the hill to fetch a pail of water,
Jack fell down and broke his crown and Jill came
   tumbling after.
But Jack and Rose, I will suppose, climb up the hill in
   laughter.
They laugh and sing till the steeples ring, and live
   happily ever after.

"He was a poet as well as a scientist," she added.

"Yes!" he said. "Yes! But do you know, did he have another name? Jack what? Do you know?"

"Jack Gibbs. It's written on his picture."

"Jack Gibbs." All three of the hill people repeated the name as though it meant magic. "Jack Gibbs."

"And you say there is a picture of him. Have you got the picture?" the old woman asked, just as eager as the man now.

"In my satchel," Rose said, and then Jacob had to run to fetch the satchel which he had left with the rubbish to be taken away to Martyn's compost yard.

After a few anxious moments, he came back with it, and Rose found the crumpled photograph stuck to the bottom of it in a mess of squashed apple pulp. The old woman wiped it clean, and there was Grandfather's face, creased but still recognizable, and there was his name written on the back.

"She's Jack Gibbs' granddaughter!" the old woman said, and began to cry again.

All this crying! Rose thought and frowned at her.

"And don't you look at me like that, my girl," the

old woman said to her. "Aw! Look at her, Idris!" she said to the man. "She's just like our Gibbs when she scowls like that."

"Who is this Gibbs? And what is all this crying for?" Rose was beginning to think that it was time they explained a few things to her. "All this about Rose, sweet Rose, with the golden hound, and now Grandfather too. Tell me!" she demanded.

"You grandmother never taught you 'please' by the sound of it," the old woman grumbled, but the man, Idris, began to explain it all to her.

"It all began a long time ago," he told her.

"When Things Went Wrong," Rose said.

"Yes, when things went wrong...Your grandfather was a very, very clever man, a physicist. That's a kind of scientist," he explained to her as he saw her look puzzled. "He was one of a group of scientists who had predicted that things were going to go wrong, but no one listened...until it was too late, and the grass had begun to die.

"The climate, and the weather, changed completely. Terrible storms began, dry storms with no rain but fierce winds which had come down from high in the sky where they had always used to blow. There were earthquakes too, and tidal waves, and for a while it seemed that Earth herself was going to disintegrate. People began to fight. People always fight when it's a matter of survival. Earth was in chaos.

"And then Jack Gibbs gathered a group of his friends, all good scientists...more physicists, chemists, biologists, doctors of medicine, climatologists...He gathered them and brought them to this hill."

"And his brother?" Rose asked. "Grandmother said he had a brother."

"Yes, his brother came too. His brother was an expert in agriculture. And they all began to try to find out if there was anything they could do to put things right again. And we think—*Gibbs* thinks—that they would have, if Jack Gibbs hadn't gone away."

"He went to save Grandmother," Rose said.

"Yes, he heard that this girl—the girl he planned to marry—hadn't been killed in the fighting, as he had been told, but was alive somewhere out in the old industrial area on the sea marshes. So he went to fetch her. But he never came back, and without him the research program came to an end." Idris waved his hand expressively. "It simply fizzled out. They needed his brain. But he didn't come back. He let them down—or so Gibbs believes."

"He had Grandmother, and my father a Baby," Rose explained. "And then the snow came, and then he was killed. He told Grandmother to come here, but she couldn't, but now I've come instead."

"Yes," Idris said. "Now you've come, Rose, with your golden hound. Tell me, did you follow our light? Your grandfather arranged with his brother to always shine the light in the hours of darkness—most hours in fact, in this perpetual Winter."

"I did follow it," Rose said.

"We knew you would!" Jacob, who had been listening intently, now had to join in. "We've got a song about you, only we always thought it was about a golden hound with a flower called a rose in its mouth. We thought when the hound with the rose came, Summer would come back, or, at least, that something special would happen. That is, *we* thought that, but Gibbs never did. Do you think Gibbs might believe it now that Rose is a person?" he asked Idris.

Idris looked at Rose. "It would do Gibbs good to believe

in something like the fulfillment of a legend, instead of staying immersed in research, research, nothing but research," he said. "You came for help." He looked at Rose thoughtfully. "I have a feeling that if you yourself ask Gibbs for help, not only will *you* get help, but you could help Gibbs too." He stood up. "She's going to see Gibbs herself," he told the old woman. "Bring the picture, and call your hound to follow," he told Rose, and he scooped her up in his arms and swept out of the room.

The tower seemed to Rose to be a huge hut. In fact, it seemed to be hut after hut after hut, as Idris carried her from one room to another, and up flight after flight of stairs. And all those people! There were men and women dressed in long gowns and slippers, like Toad in the book. And the children! There *must* be a school on the hill! Rose was sure that she saw at least a hundred children, and all of them gazing at her and Gyp and whispering her name. "Rose! Sweet Rose has come."

At last, Idris stopped outside a door. "Have you got the photo ready?" he asked Rose.

"Photo?"

"The picture—have it ready." He knocked on the door. They listened. Someone was arguing... quarrelling. Rose heard loud voices.

"*Allowing* this superstition of golden dogs bringing roses in Winter is one thing," a voice was saying, "but *believing* that this child is the fulfillment of the legend is another. And as for allowing it to persuade me to rescue some poor savage from the Camps... Well, Anne, really!" Idris knocked again. "Come!" the voice said.

"Right! Now or never! You're on your own, Rose," Idris said.

On her own! Of course she was on her own. Fancy thinking he had to tell her that! She was always on her own, really, and she always had been. Rose thought that Idris was being stupid again, as he carried her into the room and set her down on her feet in front of Gibbs.

And Gibbs was a woman. A tall, strong, brown, very clever woman. The sort of woman Rose would be herself one day. But whereas Rose always had warmth and compassion as well as strength of mind, Gibbs was cold. She stood now, one hand placed lightly on her hip, and surveyed Rose.

"Rose, sweet Rose, that comes in Winter," she said wearily.

Cue! Gibbs sounded like Grandmother did when she wanted Rose to sing to her.

Rose sang:

Rose, sweet Rose, that comes in Winter
To warm my heart and still my tears.
Come with your golden hound. Bring Summer
To this lone hill in these troubled years.

Gibbs listened. "Well! And who taught you that?" she asked sarcastically, raising her eyebrows and glancing at Jacob's mother.

"Grandmother," Rose said.

Gibbs was surprised.

"She's Jack Gibbs' granddaughter," Idris said. "She has a photograph of him."

Gibbs held out her hand, and, prodded forward by Idris, Rose handed her the picture. She looked at it for a long time. Then she sighed. "Why yes, dear Uncle Jack, so it is," she said.

"Uncle?" Rose asked. It was another new word.

"Your grandfather was my father's brother," Gibbs told her. "Big deal for both of us, Rose, I'm afraid."

She looked at the photo again. "What else did your grand-mother teach you to sing?" she asked.

Rose sang the Jack and Rose song.

Gibbs sneered. It made her look ugly. "Another of Jack's masterpieces by the sound of it. He should have stayed *here* and worked, not gone off on some fool trip to waste himself on some girl he met on a mountain." She sounded angry. "Jack Gibbs...a brain Mankind could have benefitted from for years. Years! And he goes off to try to save some illiterate shop girl."

"Illiterate?" Another new word...and it didn't sound nice. "What's illiterate?" Rose turned to ask Idris.

Idris was upset. He shrugged his shoulders and shook his head and waved his hands vaguely. "It means... means she can't read," he said.

"Grandmother *can* read. *I* can read!" Rose had known that they were running her down again. She would show them! She would remember what she could read. She would remember some of Grandmother's book. She stood there, looking through the window of the room at the silver sky. Her head was beginning to hurt again now that she was standing up. But she would remember. She began: "The mole had been working very hard all the morning spring-cleaning his little home."

"It's *The Wind in the Willows*," Jacob's mother said. "You know *The Wind in the Willows*!"

Rose nodded. Oh, how her head was hurting! But she would carry on. She shut her eyes. What came next? "Today the snow began. The temperature outside my laboratory here in this hole beneath the power station is minus twenty-one degrees Fahrenheit..." She stopped. That wasn't right. She began again. "We thought that we had a hundred years to prepare for this Ice Age, but now, through our own foolish, uncoordinated actions,

which I have listed, we have brought about disaster..."
It still wasn't right. It was the Voice words she was
remembering. The awful Voice! Rose opened her eyes
and looked around in anguish.

But what was happening? Gibbs was on her knees,
tense with interest. "Is that from a book? Have you
another book out there in The Camps?"

Rose tried to shake her head. She almost fell. Gibbs
caught her and sat her on a chair.

"Now, Rose, *sweet* Rose, tell me about *those* words,"
she begged.

So Rose told Gibbs all about the Voice in the Hole,
about the storms and the Sparking Place, about Grandfather's Rules and the Bosses' Rules, about wailing—
and about that final, fatal afternoon.

Gibbs stood up and pressed the palms of her hands
against her forehead. "Jack Gibbs' voice on a video! Jack
Gibbs' voice! *Pray* that that video machine was not
damaged in that explosion. Pray!" she said passionately.
"*Dear* Uncle Jack! Pray that he left enough information
for me to finish his work. And how *exactly* did he harness
the storms? How did he set that machine? And how
did he make it stay working all these years? I must
know that too..." She gave her orders. "We'll use the
Craft. We'll go today. There should be enough light."

Grandfather's voice. It was Grandfather's voice, and
Grandmother had never told her. Rose couldn't believe
it. But what was all this about "the Craft"?

"What does she mean?" Rose looked at Idris.

"She means that we will go to rescue your grandmother
and the baby," he told her. Then he smiled sadly at Gibbs.
"Though not from the noblest of motives, my love," he
said to her.

"Idris," Gibbs answered coldly. "It takes Martyn twelve months to manufacture enough gas for a journey such as this. I cannot afford to waste it because of sentiment about one old Camps woman, no matter who she is — nor to satisfy a superstitious legend," she said. "But to fetch a video of Jack Gibbs' work — *that* is an entirely different matter."

Idris shook his head. "Gibbs," he said, "*I* shall pray that Sweet Rose will one day teach you the difference between sentimentality and compassion, for that day she will indeed have fulfilled the legend, and brought warmth where it is so desperately needed."

15
Camp Again

They took Rose with them. They had to, to show them
the way. There were so many Camps, and all of them
were hostile. They wrapped her in a soft shawl, and
dressed themselves in trousers and jackets, and fastened
warm cloaks around their shoulders. They armed themselves, too, with small blow-pipes, each one fitted, ready
with a dart, its tip wet with some substance they warned
Rose not to touch. Gyp stayed with her pups and Jacob,
but Martyn came with them, and so did three other
strong, hard-looking men, as well as Idris. Gibbs led.

The Craft was like a low-ceilinged hut. It roared like
thunder, and Rose covered her ears with the shawl as
they sped above the plain, following the river at first,
then branching off, out across the barren, brown soil.
There was the pine tree! Rose pointed it out. Gibbs swung
the Craft slightly, and sped towards it. There were the
towers.

"There!" Rose said, and pointed at the hut.

"But it's right in the middle of the old power station!"
one of the men said. "Only a fool would make a Camp
there."

"A fool...or a very clever physicist who knew how
to use the old Station to generate power for his laboratory
from the storms," Gibbs said. "Yes, a very clever
physicist."

Rats scattered as the Craft nosed its way between
the towers, avoiding the twisted rails and the hanging

cables. Gibbs stopped it in the space between the hut and the Hole. They made Rose stay inside it with Martyn to make sure that she stayed there, while Gibbs and the three strong men began to force their way, with great care, beneath the wreckage that covered The Hole, and Idris went into the hut.

He stayed inside it for a very long time. Rose fretted. She rocked in her seat, to and fro, to and fro. When would he come out again? What was he doing?

When he came out he held, tenderly in his arms, a small bundle of soft, wolf skins. "Baby!" Rose began to relax... but then she noticed Idris's bowed head, and the way he would not look at her.

He laid Baby in her arms without a word, turning away quickly. "Come with me," he said to Martyn. "Bring a blanket."

Martyn pulled a roll of soft, brown cloth from beneath his seat and followed him. Rose looked at Baby.

"Aw...aah..." She stopped her wail quickly. No Boss. No wailing... but Baby was nearly gone! He was lasting, but only just...Why was he so still? She had forgotten how thin he was. "Baby, Baby," she crooned to him and began to rock in her seat again.

As though he knew her voice, Baby turned his face towards her and opened his eyes. He did know her! He smiled and squirmed appreciatively. She put her little finger inside his fist and helped him pull it to his mouth. A washed finger! He would like that...but would he last?

"You must last, you *must*," she told him. "Listen! I'm going to give you your name. Then you *must* last... You are...you are..." What should she call him? Jack! "You are Jack!" she said.

And then she looked up and saw Grandmother. She pressed Baby to her and watched helplessly as Martyn carried the old woman from the hut. Bones! She was nothing but bones and yellow skin. She was going. But she wasn't like this when I left! What happened? I left food. Didn't she eat?..."You didn't eat!" she snarled at her as they laid her in the aisle between the seats, with a folded blanket beneath her head, and more tucked in around her.

"I did, I did!" Grandmother said.

"She got cold," Iris said quietly, "far too cold."

"You let the fire go out!" Rose snarled at her again.

"No...no!" Grandmother was distressed. "I went out." She tried to smile, and coughed painfully.

"You went *out*!" Rose couldn't believe it. "Why? Why? Why?"

"Didn't think you'd get back with help," Grandmother said. Her voice was weak. Rose had to lean down close to hear her. "Didn't think a load of scientists would bother with an old bag of bones like me...Just my luck they did!" She coughed again.

Rose looked away. "She's *going*!" she snarled at Idris. "Do something, you *scientist*! Do something. Help!"

Idris simply shook his head, and took Baby from her and began to wrap him in a shawl.

Then Gibbs came back, triumphant, glowing, with the small, gray video box in her arms. Grandmother had been right. That was the important thing.

"You were right." Rose bent over Grandmother. "You were right about the small box."

"Grandfather told me," she said.

"They know about Grandfather," Rose told her. "The Voice is him, isn't it. You never told me."

Grandmother smiled sadly. "I might have, one day, but I was afraid of what Boss would do if he found out..." She closed her eyes.

Rose talked frantically. "They know our song, too. And they know your book. We can read your book all day now."

Grandmother's face contorted with sudden worry. She opened her eyes again. "I hid the book. That's why I went out—to hide the book safe from rats and Bosses, to hide it safe..."

The Craft engine was starting. They were moving. "Where...where?"

Rose was frantic. "We must take it. Where...where?"

"In Jack's secret...the pine tree..."

Rose pushed her way past the men to Gibbs. "Stop!" She pulled her arm. "Stop! The book, she hid her book."

Gibbs didn't stop. The Craft glided forward. "It's only an ordinary old book," she said. "It doesn't matter."

"It does! It does! She hid it at the pine tree. She hid it safe from rats and Bosses."

Slowly, Gibbs realized exactly what Rose was telling her. "Do you mean that that arthritic, old woman made herself move between that hut and the pine tree? All that way—to make sure that a book was safe? All that way! The pain!" She looked down at Grandmother. "The original Rose," she said. "Yes, we will stop."

Gibbs stopped the Craft at the hummock, and she and Rose scrambled out together. Rose remembered that she had left the secret place open. Grandmother hadn't had to lift the stone. That had helped. But she had shut it down again. Now Gibbs lifted it, and then, as Rose picked up the book, Gibbs stood with her back to the pine tree, as Rose used to do—as Grandmother and Jack Gibbs had once done—and she began to understand. She looked across the plain to the hill, where the light had begun to shine as the hours of darkness came near. Then she looked back at the camp, with the sky behind it streaked with purple...and then she looked down at Rose with the book in her hands. *"The Wind in the Willows,"* she said. "A tale of genteel, civilized animals... I was wrong about your grandmother, Rose. She is a sensible, brave woman, and well worth saving. She kept in touch with civilization through this book, and stopped you from becoming a complete and utter savage. We must take care of this book, for her sake, forever."

She took Rose's hand in hers and ran back to the Craft and lifted her inside, and they began the journey to the hill.

But Grandmother never reached the hill. When Rose saw the willows on the banks of the river, she remembered how she had planned to tell her all about them. Now she wouldn't have to. Grandmother could see them for herself. She made Gibbs stop the Craft again. And Martyn lifted Grandmother, tenderly, and she died there, in his arms, looking at willow trees.

Next day they came back and they buried Grandmother beneath the willow trees. They built a cairn of stones above her grave, a huge cairn which they could see clearly from the hill, so that every time they looked out towards the Camps, they would remember her.

Rose was very bitter. "You were so close, by Craft! You could have come to us. You could have stopped us being cold. You could have stopped us starving. You could have helped us last...Why didn't you come to help?" she stormed at Gibbs.

"Rose, Rose! Think about it," Gibbs said patiently. "We haven't always had the Craft."

"Well, why didn't you come on the horses? You could have come in a day, not a week, on horses."

"We couldn't have come on horses through the Snow, Rose. The Snow lasted twenty years, you know—and after that we thought Jack Gibbs and your grandmother must be dead."

"You could have come to find out. Why didn't you come to find out?"

"Because we couldn't afford to lose any more of us," Gibbs said. "A lot of hill people died, too, during the Snow, and when it went we found that we were only going to be safe if we stayed here and turned the hill into a fortress. We had to keep our work safe too, you see. Our work is very important, Rose. We couldn't — and we still can't — risk having it all destroyed by a mob of murderous savages."

Rose thought of Boss and Gyp's old master, and knew that Gibbs could be right, but she still argued. "But we were not all savages in the Camps."

"But we didn't know that."

"Well, you should have come and found out," Rose said, and to that Gibbs had no answer.

16
The Future

But there was someone who did try to find out more about the Camps, and that was young Jack—Baby.

Idris, who was a medical scientist, and the new Grandmother took over Baby when they brought him to the hill. For weeks they devoted every minute of the day and the night to looking after him, and he survived, or, as Rose said, "he lasted."

As he grew up he wanted to know all about himself, and Rose told him about the Camps, and, when he was about seventeen, he decided that he wanted to go and see them for himself, so she gave him Grandfather's knife and the survival bag, and he went off, with Finn, one of Gyp's grandsons, at his heels.

He came back a month later with a boy about his own age who wanted a dog like Finn... but that's another story.

And Rose? Well, she was never ever really "sweet." She was kind and sensible and loving, but much too tough ever to be described honestly as "sweet." She did, however, seem to make people happy—even Gibbs.

Gibbs took her to live with her, and brought her up as though she was her own daughter. She would have liked Rose to have been a physicist, like herself, but Rose was not really interested, so Gibbs trained her, instead, to take over her role as Leader at the hill, while Jacob came to work with her in the laboratory in the tower beneath the bright light.

Rose was the best Leader the hill ever had. This was partly because the people loved her as Sweet Rose, who had come to fulfill their legend, even though the scientists had told them it was all superstitious nonsense. But they *liked* her too, because, unlike Gibbs and her father before her, Rose thought that people didn't have to be scientists to be important at the hill. "Everybody can be good at something," was Rose's Rules, for she remembered that even poor, hated Boss had been very good at hunting wolves.

And she did bring Summer, though not for many, many years after she had gone. Because of the video of Jack Gibbs's work which she had brought Gibbs to find, the scientists at the hill discovered exactly why everything had gone wrong. Gibbs studied the video for several weeks, and then she called a meeting of everyone on the hill so that she could explain it to them. Gibbs had never called a meeting like this before, and everyone was astonished, until she told them that Jack Gibbs had told her to call it, on his video. Then the Grandmother, and one or two of the other, older people, understood, for they could remember Jack Gibbs. "He wasn't like his brother and the others," they said. "When you were chatting with him, you always forgot that he wasn't one of us."

They met in the round hall, halfway up the tower. Rose loved this bright hall, with its round table and huge, square windows through which she could see the pine tree and her Camp, now that she had learned exactly where to look. Idris told her to sit on the stool next to the big, throne-like chair which belonged to Gibbs, the Leader, and when Gibbs came and sat in this chair Rose was the first to notice that she had brought a small, gray, metal box with her which looked unpleasantly similar to the gray box from the Hole. For a moment, Rose felt uncomfortable. But Gibbs placed the box on the table in front of her and ignored it as she began to speak to them.

And what Gibbs told them was even more astonishing to them than the fact that she had called a meeting, for Gibbs told them that the catastrophic change in Earth's climate, which Rose called "When Things Went Wrong," and they called "Earthchange," had not been something that Earth did to them, but something that they did to Earth. In fact, that people had made it happen.

"In the Old Days," Gibbs said, "scientists discovered ways of changing the weather. At first it was only scientists who used this new knowledge, but, inevitably, it fell into the wrong hands, and a group of unscrupulous men began changing the weather whenever they were asked, by whoever would pay them the highest price for their 'service.' They were completely irresponsible and reckless in the things they began to do, and Jack Gibbs, and some of his friends, became extremely worried about the outcome of this wanton interference with Earth's established patterns. Jack Gibbs argued that it was folly to make rain where rain should not be, to divert hurricanes from the path they were intended to follow, to make snow fall out of season. And he calculated that, in a hundred years, this deliberate interference would bring about disaster.

"He tried to persuade Earth's leaders to pass laws to make it illegal..."

Grandfather's Rules! Rose thought.

"...but Earth's leaders preferred to listen to those scientists who disagreed with him.

"It was at this point that he asked his friends to come and work with him on this hill. Together they observed and researched and experimented, and they, too, calculated that disaster was inevitable, but not at once. Like him they thought we had a hundred years' grace.

"But disaster came within months, not even years, and we have never been able to understand why. Why did the decline in the quality of Earth's climate accelerate? We have asked ourselves that question ever since." Gibbs paused. "Jack Gibbs discovered why."

Suddenly Rose realized that Gibbs was agitated. She was tapping the table nervously with her fingertips. But she went on talking. "The fact that Jack Gibbs should discover this answer is extremely interesting to me," Gibbs said, "for I have calculated the chance, the probability, of his doing so in this way, and it is extremely low indeed." Suddenly she faltered. She sat there, her lips parted slightly, gazing through the square window opposite her at a point somewhere high in the silver sky. "It is so low, so improbable, that I feel it wasn't just *chance*. It was *luck*. But I don't *believe* in luck. And it's so *fair* that *he* should discover it, because he did so deserve to, that I feel it was *justice*. But I don't believe in justice either. Luck and justice are just things of the mind." She was arguing with herself. She looked confused. "It's this hill," she said, "this hill with its superstitions and its mysteries. It defies logic...O-oh, we need a philosopher, we do so need a philosopher!" She pressed her hand over her eyes for a moment, but only for a moment. Her confusion soon passed, and then she went on in her usual factual, forthright way. "Jack Gibbs left his work here unfinished to go to the Camps to save the girl who became Rose's grandmother. And, in doing so, he met the one man left on Earth who could tell him about the final, fatal act of interference with the weather. At the Camps he met a man whom he describes as the boss of the muscle-men employed by the group..."

First Boss! Boss's father! Rose listened intently.

"This man was their sole survivor. He was not clever, but he was able to tell Jack Gibbs exactly what had happened." Gibbs looked ugly with cynicism and anger. "Their final 'service to Mankind' had been to use an atomic explosion to break off a large portion of the icecap on Earth's northern polar region, and to float it halfway across Earth's oceans to flood a desert in what was then one of her hot, dry places. But the moment this vast island of ice began to drift south, came chaos. The jet stream, of winds faster than the hurricanes in our storms, descended from the stratosphere where it belongs. It swept seas across continents and left them there as ice. It caused eruptions and earthquakes of great magnitude. And, then it swept back up again, carrying with it clouds of white dust which it deposited in the atmosphere, to whirl, endlessly, between us and the sun. This chaos was Earthchange."

Rose was beginning to feel bewildered. Earthchange ...Earthchange...When Things Went Wrong...And it had been First Boss who had done it! Well, he was one of the ones. *The* one as far as she was concerned. And Grandfather had found out. And if Grandfather had known about him, then so must have Grandmother. Another secret!

Everyone had begun to talk, and soon, inevitably, came the question: "And does Jack Gibbs tell you how to make things go right again?" Martyn asked it.

"He does," Gibbs said, and then she smiled sarcastically. "You will all be expecting a miracle, of course, but there will be no miracle. There will be hard work, for me...and for you."

"What?" they said. "Us work as scientists?"

"No. We will each work at our own profession. Jack Gibbs has laid down a pattern which I shall follow to complete his research. I can do that now that he has sent the relevant fact concerning the last stage in the Earthchange process. He has also set a program for my horticulturalist colleagues and the chemists among us. But it is to you, the people, that he gives the most important task. He said you were to be told that, by the way. He said that we scientists were to be quite honest with you. He said that we must tell you that there is nothing *we* can do to repair the damage that has been done to Earth's climate, and that what *we*, all of us, have to do is work to help Earth repair her climate for herself."

"How...how?" they asked.

"Basically, by planting trees and grass. Yes, it's as simple as that — or it would be if we didn't have this infernal cold and wet. But I shall let Jack Gibbs tell you about that himself," she said, and then she leaned forward and switched on the video.

The Voice rang out.

Rose sat quite still, biting her lip and gripping the edges of her stool until her fingers hurt. Would they wail? Would these people wail?

Of course, they people of the hill didn't wail. They listened sensibly. And, when Rose realized there would be no wail, she grew calmer, she relaxed, and she began to listen too, and there was nothing frightening about the Voice at all. It was simply the voice of Jack Gibbs, *her* Grandfather, the scientist, telling them how to Make Things Go Right.

She heard him talk of sowing new pastures and creating wildernesses, of making oceans clean and rivers flow with fresh water. She heard him talk of "restoring Earth's natural balance and variety" and "developing a means of worldwide communication and cooperation with other groups such as your own." Jack Gibbs the scientist was teaching them.

But, towards the end, it wasn't Jack Gibbs the scientist but Jack Gibbs the poet who began to speak, and Jack Gibbs the poet spoke of green hills, of fields golden with ripening corn, of gardens fragrant with flowers, of wildernesses rich with a variety of other animals, of woodlands jubilant with the song of birds. Rose knew every word by heart. She joined in with them, and suddenly they were wonderful.

And when they were finished, Gibbs switched off the video, and that was the last time Rose ever heard the Voice, for Gibbs locked it away with the rest of her work. Gibbs was determined that, from now on, that video was going to be part of her scientific program. No one was ever going to turn it into the Voice again.

The information and advice on it was invaluable. Gibbs and her fellow scientists, and Martyn and his farmers and gardeners, began using it right away. Jacob took over from Gibbs when she died, and Martyn's daughter took over from him, and their children took over in their turn and so did their children after them. And, after many, many years, the work of Jack Gibbs the scientist made the words of Jack Gibbs the poet come true, for Earth became warm and fertile and beautiful again. Sweet Rose *had* brought Summer to the hill.